The Absent Shakespeare

The Absent Shakespeare

Mark Jay Mirsky

Rutherford • Madison • Teaneck
Fairleigh Dickinson University Press
London and Toronto: Associated University Presses

Associated University Presses
440 Forsgate Drive
Cranbury, NJ 08512

Associated University Presses
25 Sicilian Avenue
London WC1A 2QH, England

Associated University Presses
P.O. Box 338, Port Credit
Mississauga, Ontario
Canada L5G 4L8

The paper used in this publication meets the requirements
of the American National Standard for Permanence of Paper
for Printed Library Materials Z39.48-1984.

Linocut illustrations by Inger Johanne Grytting.

Library of Congress Cataloging-in-Publication Data

Mirsky, Mark Jay, 1939–
  The absent Shakespeare / Mark Jay Mirsky ; [linocut illustrations
by Inger Johanne Grytting].
    p.   cm.
  Includes bibliographical references (p.) and index.
  ISBN 0-8386-3511-3 (alk. paper)
    1. Shakespeare, William, 1564–1616—Knowledge—Psychology.
2. Characters and characteristics in literature.   3. Shakespeare,
William, 1564–1616—Characters.   4. Parent and child in literature
5. Psychoanalysis and literature.   6. Psychology in literature.
  I. Title.
PR3065.M57   1994
822.3'3—dc20   92-55118
                                                                   CIP

PRINTED IN THE UNITED STATES OF AMERICA

For Mary K
Beloved Provocateur

Contents

Bibliographical Note

IN the case of *King Lear*, all quotes are from *The Parallel King Lear*, prepared by Michael Warren (Berkeley: University of California Press, 1989), which prints in photographic facsimile, the First Folio of 1623 on pages facing the First Quarto of 1608. Where Warren provides corrected readings in his margin, I have adopted them. Warren gives absolute line counts, rather than using the device of act, scene, line number (within the scene). To simplify the task of the reader wishing to check the text against other editions I have usually followed the convention of giving acts and scenes for both folio and quarto references, with the absolute line numbers separated from the former by a colon. The text of *Hamlet* in the Folio is from *The Norton Facsimile: The First Folio of Shakespeare*, edited by Charlton Hinman (New York: W. W. Norton, 1968), cited as *FF.*; the First Quarto of 1603 from the Shakespeare Quarto Facsimiles, no. 7 (Oxford: At the Clarendon Press, n.d.,) cited as *Q1.*, and the Second Quarto of 1604–1605, from the collotype facsimile edition of Oxford University Press (reprinted 1964), cited as *Q2.* Act, scene, and line numbers in the Second Quarto are copied from *Hamlet*, (Harmondsworth: Pelican, 1970), edited by William Farnham. For *Macbeth,* I have used the Folger Library edition edited by Louis B. Wright and Virginia A. LaMar (1959), which is based on the Folio of 1623 and for *The Tempest*, the New Penguin edition of 1987, edited by Anne Righter, also based on the Folio of 1623.

The scholarly reader may find my spelling eccentric. I have modernized spelling through the texts of *King Lear* and *Hamlet* wherever this did not seem to change stage pronunciation. The peculiarities of the Elizabethan usage suggest in some cases elongated pronunciation, but,wherever I could clarify the text without damage to what might have been a deliberate difference between modern and Shakespearean usage, I did. In a few cases where folio or quarto punctuation needed clarification, I added my own in square brackets. Turned up or turned under lines are not indicated. It seemed to me as a novelist who was once an actor and director that the capitalization suggested emphasis and that it was unwise to omit it. If Shakespeare had a hand in the folio revisions, capitals may have been a means, like the folio's punctuation and abbreviation, of indicating subtleties of delivery. I do not, as the reader will note, draw any conclusions however, in these essays, from capitalization or abbreviation. For *Macbeth* and *The Tempest*, I depended on the choices of the editors of the Pelican and Penguin editions, respectively.

Acknowledgments

I would like to acknowledge the support of my editor, Harry Key-ishian, as well as my colleagues at The City College of New York, Leo Hamalian, Edward Quinn, and Steven Urkowitz. All were more than generous with time and suggestions.

My debts run back to Harvard College where Reuben Brower, Harry Levin, Alfred Harbage, Alan Lebowitz, and Larry Friedlander made Shakespeare and the Elizabethans a vivid, living experience; to many conversations with my friend and teacher, William Alfred, and to Albert Guerard. The latter insisted I take my students to the stage when I taught under his aegis at Stanford University.

My students, Allan Aycock, Irene Szeto, and Erica Obey, helped check pages fraught with questions and my wife, Inger, not only provided prints for the book, but patiently read through the chapters many times. Ross Wetzsteon at *The Village Voice,* one of the first readers of the completed manuscript, gave me his discriminating enthusiasm and found a place in that publication for its arguments.

The Absent Shakespeare

1

The Absent Shakespeare

HAMLET and *King Lear*!

These two engines rise above the mechanical claptrap of stage devices and furniture to batter through the doors of dreams. Profound, unsettling dramas, they challenge biblical narrative as sacred text. The atmosphere of the uncanny hangs over them, as if in their lines the unfolding of our own lives could be read, a prophecy of what is to come. From his perspective, Jorge Luis Borges gives a succinct statement of Shakespeare's absence from his own text: "There was no one in him; behind his face (which even through the bad paintings of those times resembles no other) and his words, which were copious, fantastic and stormy, there was only a bit of coldness, a dream dreamt by no one." With this impresario of absence, present only in his creations, the "Holy One" of Borges commiserates, "Neither am I anyone; I have dreamt the world as you dreamt your work, my Shakespeare, and among the forms in my dream are you, who like myself are many and no one."[1]

I see the opposite—the absolute of autobiography in Shakespeare's dramas, *Hamlet* and *King Lear*. I am not speaking of reconstructing the life of a man who lived in the late sixteenth, early seventeenth century, one whose mother died in 1608, and whose father in 1601.[2] (These however, make interesting bookends since it is supposed that *Hamlet* was written in 1601 and 1602, and *Lear* in 1605 or 1606.) I am thinking of Shakespeare's dream life, his obsessions, what made him unique just as the Unknown, should it exist, must be unique.[3] The psychology of God, His dreams, was Shakespeare's (as it is properly our) deepest concern—the meaning, the end of what we are about. Gloucester cries out in *King Lear* the common fear of man: "As Flies to wanton Boys, are we to th'Gods, / They kill us for their sport" (the First Folio of 1623, afterwards, *FF*.4.1: 2221–22).[4] Yet Shakespeare's fear is deeper, more personal. I do not disagree with the "sense of" absence that

15

Borges points to, but may regard it as a ploy, not an absolute condition. Absence is something expected in a hack writer, the mark of a glib professionalism that allows him to spin off stories in which he has no real interest, nothing of himself at stake. Absence in a great writer's work is the sign of a presence concealed. It is not Shakespeare's absence in *King Lear* and *Hamlet* but his dreams, his fantasies, especially as they touch the riddle of fathers, mothers, and children, that set these two plays apart. Closest to them is *The Tempest* in which the omnipotent father looms. If Ariel and Caliban are the wizard's spiritual children, their bondage despite the foolery of a comedy has a force more ominous than is perhaps intended or that the happy ending can comfortably bear.

The dark comedies, however, finally pretend to resolve their riddles. They can not leave them as pointers, disquieting, to the author's fears. In tragedies such as *Othello* and *Coriolanus* circumstance and human passion rule. One does not have that shadow dance of which Yeats sang—"Hamlet and Lear are gay; Gaiety transfiguring all that dread"—in which the playwright slips away from the action, to regard himself as a man in the grip of his obsession, acting it out. This is the mark of self-analysis, the laughter that Yeats heard as Lear sang, skipping on his bed of nails: "I will be Jovial" (*FF*.4.6: 2642). It eludes Macbeth who only sees himself acting although the distance between himself and his acts widens in his consciousness as the play goes on. His exclamation at the end, "It is a tale / told by an idiot, full of sound and fury, / signifying nothing" (5.5.28–30).[5] is not, even in the hands of a rogue actor, going to be "Jovial," jocular, but must remain agonized. Nor does Ariel's song of a "sea-change / Into something rich and strange" penetrate the world weary shell of Prospero's ear. There is no tragedy (unless it be the passage of time) in *The Tempest*, therefore no direct cry from the playwright.

The doom of *King Lear* and *Hamlet* gave Shakespeare the liberty to be personal about his dreams, to suggest a hidden text. At pains to conceal the riddle, the playwright has succeeded insofar as the force of his confession is felt, even when it is not admitted to in its inevitable misreadings—the prerequisite of its production on the stage. The naked stance behind the shadow play of kings and princes might have evoked a storm of stones: playwright and actors committed. Even today the themes are akin to the fantasies of insanity, and I approve Coleridge's paraphrase of Dryden, in penetrating Shakespeare: "Great wit to madness nearly is allied."[6]

From the asides and parenthesis, already, it must be apparent to the reader that I recognize not one *Lear*, but two, the "Quarto" text of 1608, and the "Folio" of 1623. In *Hamlet,* as well, disparities between two quarto and one folio texts necessitate a double, even a triple vision.[7] The arguments to follow were developed in the first draft of the manuscript without regard to differences between quarto and folio. The presence of Shakespeare as editor, revising from earlier quartos to a final folio version of both *King Lear* and *Hamlet* seems more plausible, however, with each reading of the plays. Persuasive demonstrations have gone before me, and the support my first ideas find in the thesis that Shakespeare revised his own plays, confirms my belief. In search of the playwright through these dramas, the dangerous riddles of his career, the opportunity to observe him reflecting, changing through reflection, his own text, is a "godsend." The notion of an "unaware" Shakespeare with which T. S. Eliot twitted a modern audience several decades past becomes even less tenable if Shakespeare revised— and revised shrewdly.

As literary texts, the quarto *King Lear* and the second quarto *Hamlet* are too compelling to suffer condescension. Not just lines, but scenes of genius would be reft from our consciousness in which the moment of drama in *Hamlet* or *King Lear* has stood for our own. While I argue for the superiority of the folio versions on the stage, I could make a case for the quarto *Lear* and second quarto *Hamlet* as the better. They are the dramas of a younger poet with flamboyant touches, more exuberant passion. I wish to distinguish, on the advice of a "better and an older" scholar, between the texts as literature and in performance. Staged distinctly and searched for their distinctions, they might be performed back to back. Multiple readings in *Hamlet* and *Lear* are appropriate to texts the fundamental ambiguity of which mirrors the riddles of lines that shift meaning with each reader and on each reading, not to mention production and performance. We too exist in time, and the plays appear to us in this looking glass. Is that why I now favor the *King Lear* and *Hamlet* as Shakespeare might last have seen them?

The folio *Lear* and *Hamlet* not only intensify the "pace" of the dramatic action, but also go the quick and deep of the playwright's self-examination in time. Shakespeare was a critic. The essays he left us are his revisions. In this self-criticism, Shakespeare reveals himself.

2

All the King's Daughters

KING Lear is a story of a dying man's desire for his daughters. The mistake made in almost all productions is in the casting of the daughters. There is no cleavage of age such as often appears in the casting of the sisters; the audience sees a young Cordelia, an only moderately attractive Regan, and a mature dowager, Gonerill. But the daughters are all young, too young. Lear is a king who has created children in old age, children who are his grandchildren, as has his mirror image, Gloucester. Cordelia is an adolescent. Her outburst, her sulking silence, is the attractive but infuriating budding of sexual desire toward which the old King, dying, instinctively gropes. He has no real wish to give Cordelia, her "young love," to suitors, either the clinging embrace implicit in "The Vines of France" or the cowish Duke characterized through the "Milk of Burgundy" (*FF.*1.1: 90) as timorous and fearful—and so he proves. These last lines are all additions of the Folio, of Shakespeare in maturity, to whom sexual tensions will be paramount. The Quarto of 1608 gave *King Lear* a strong political bent, justifying the Duke of Albany's wavering in loyalty to the cause of King Lear by referring to the threat to England from France. In the later Folio, the lines of justification are largely omitted. "The elaborate excuse that Albany is morally bound to defend England against the 'foreign invader' vanishes from the Folio. In fact, with the exception of Cornwall's announcement in 3.7, 'The Army of France is landed,' every reference to Cordelia's army as being French has been cut from the Folio."[1] The scholar just quoted demonstrates that the cuts create a sense of "moral ambiguity" about Albany. The *additions* in the Folio, however, point to an equally ominous result in the realm of "moral ambiguity."

By splitting the kingdom in three, Lear would create a political disaster for England, weakening it irrevocably. Indeed even the twofold division with Cordelia excluded brings France, England's hereditary enemy, as "a power / Into this scattered kingdom."

(Q.3.1: 1406–07) (This line exists only in the Quarto. The Folio cuts it, but notes that the division between the Dukes has been reported by their servants who are "Spies" to France.[2])

Why? An English audience of 1605–1606 must have shuddered at Britain divided in three, especially if Cordelia's (therefore either France's or Burgundy's) is to be "A third, more opulent than your Sisters" (FF.1.1: 92), that is, sisters wedded to Englishmen. The King reveals the reason for his action, however, in his furious attack of frustrated passion in the wake of his daughter Cordelia's refusal—(refusal of what? Stay!) "I loved her most, and thought to set my rest / On her kind nursery" (FF.1.1.131–32). Where will that "nursery" be—in France? Hardly. Lear's fantasy is that Cordelia will abide, without husband, in England, tending to him, Lear: not her "nothing," but her quite specific *something*. "Happily when I shall wed, / That Lord, whose hand must take my plight, shall carry / Half my love with him, half my Care and Duty, / Sure I shall never marry like my Sisters" (FF.1.1: 107–10). The Quarto concludes with, "to love my father all" (Q.1.1: 93). This is what drives the King into fits. He has been exposed in his dream of maintaining his daughter in his grasp. The implicit promise of "half" her time is ignored, for it is the truth of Lear's desire that is suddenly in the open. His frantic indiscretions and follies in this disappointment do to him exactly what he fears most—put Cordelia completely out of his clutches and compound his mistake. Of course he does not expect France to take her. A reduced, begging Cordelia is what Lear imagines, broken and pliable, her vulnerability enhanced by the pathos of her condition.

So far the stage conventions are not much violated. A tender fourteen-year-old Cordelia can be accommodated. But this is not the end of the story Shakespeare feared to tell. He foresaw his own old age, a man overwhelmed by desire for his daughters. Gonerill and Regan, so cunning, are also pitiful, awkward. Their speeches professing love are not glib—as always performed—but halting, desperate; clichés that stop in midsentence, in nothing, in space, air, flailing, as they try to flirt with the dangerous old man. They are but paraphrases of the same "nothing"; Gonerill's "A love which makes breath poor, and speech unable" (FF.1.1: 65) echoed by Regan's "she names my very deed of love" (FF. 1.1: 76). It is the beaming face of their father asking pledges of love that unnerves his daughters. "Let Copulation thrive" (FF. 4.6: 2559) is in Lear's mind from the instant of abdication. Is he harboring the dread fantasy of a father as age strips him of artful sublimations? He is rejected first by Gonerill—a Gonerill who is nineteen or twenty bowing before him; a woman before childbirth, one whom Edmund can desire in truth and the King covet. ("Dry up in her the Organs of increase" [FF.1.4: 793] has no force if Gonerill is streaked with gray.) In his rage at being told that he is "Old and Reverend" but not "Wise" and to associate not with the "pranks" of the "debauched" but "such men as may besort your Age" (FF. 1.4: 760), and understanding the sexual condescension to him, Lear attacks his daughter's body. He *inserts* himself in a wish of rape to tear her womb. The syllables are a crowbar in his mouth.

> Suspend thy purpose, if thou didst intend
> To make this Creature fruitful:
> Into her Womb convey sterility.
> Dry up in her the Organs of increase,
> And from her derogate body, never spring
> A Babe to honor her. If she must teem,
> Create her child of Spleen, that it may live
> And be a thwart disnatured torment to her.
> Let it stamp wrinkles in her brow of youth,
> With cadent Tears fret Channels in her cheeks . . .
>
> (FF.1, 4: 790–99)

Lear's curse on his daughter's physical beauty, her "brow of youth," speaks to his admiration. This is a lover's not a father's execration—or rather a father as lover. Lear's "hot tears" flow out of control before Albany, Gonerill's husband. At the end of the foregoing tirade, there breaks from the King further confession, "I am ashamed / That thou hast power to shake my manhood thus" (FF.1.4: 815–16).

Is this love reciprocated? Do Gonerill and Regan recognize their father's claims? Their husbands do not satisfy them. Gonerill's description of her marital situation in the letter she sends to Edmund is grim: ". . . if he / return the Conqueror, then am I the Prisoner, and his bed, my / Gaol, from the loathed warmth whereof, deliver me, and sup- / ply the place for your Labor" (FF.4.6: 2718–21). To herself Gonerill muses, "My Fool usurps my body" (FF. 4.2: 2297). Regan's immediate shift of affections following her husband's murder implies, like Gertrude's in *Hamlet*, that the recent ties between herself and Cornwall have hardly been passionate. (In the Olivier production of *King Lear*, Regan looks with amused detachment on the wounded Cornwall, already dreaming of displacing him. The "Give me thy arm" of the dying Duke is mocked.) Something is amiss, troubled, their pledges of love to their father in the first scene as Cordelia divines, disgrace them. "Why have my Sisters

Husbands, if they say / They love you all?" (*FF*.1.1: 106–7). Their marriages are hollow, shadowed by the King's paternal demands and claim. The game they play with him—"Which of you shall we say doth love us most, / That we, our largest bounty may extend / Where Nature doth with merit challenge" (*FF*.1.1: 56–58) is real. This is seen in the King's explosion when his youngest will not play. It can not be the first time the children have been asked to demonstrate their "natures." Lear must have teased the daughters with his authority since the death of his wife—"I gave you all," he cries to his two older daughters. The younger, Regan, snaps back, "And in *good* time you *gave* it" (*FF*.2.4: 1547–48).

The hideous "nature" of Gonerill and Regan, their anger turning them into murderesses, their sexual hunger into adulteresses, obscures the King's behavior. Is it not possible that Lear, sensing the vacuity of their beds, comes with his hundred knights to enforce a claim to which he can not openly admit? Gonerill's complaint of orgies among Lear's followers, bears a closer look.

> Here do you keep a hundred Knights and Squires,
> Men so disorder'd, so debosh'd, and bold,
> That this our Court infected with their manners,
> Shows like a riotous Inn; Epicurism and Lust
> Makes it more like a Tavern, or a Brothel,
> Than a grac'd Palace. The shame itself doth speak
> For instant remedy.
>
> (*FF*.1.4: 750–56)

What Gonerill exaggerates of her father's debauchery and what she goes to bed and dreams of may be the same. In act 4, his social mask stripped away by rage, her father will cry out what he may well utter in the first drunken moments of retirement, relieved of responsibilities: "Too't Luxury pell-mell." The recognition, which comes after his drenching and stripping, lurked before: "Thou, Rascal Beadle, hold thy bloody / hand: why dost thou lash that Whore? Strip thy own / back, thou hotly lusts to use her in that kind, for which / thou whip'st her" (*FF*.4.6: 2603–6).

How far do they, or Cordelia, their closest kin, reciprocate? In the end, all are daughters of the same mother. The curse of the King, in his fear of Regan's rejection of his love, for she is now the youngest present, is curious. "Are you happy to see me?" is his question. But the warning slips out even as they exchange courtesies, meeting at Gloucester's castle.

Reg. I am glad to see your Highness.
Lear. Regan, I think you are. I know what reason
I have to think so, if thou should'st not be glad,
I would divorce me from thy Mother Tomb,
Sepulchering an adulteress.

(*FF.*2.4: 1406–10)

Lear's threat to name his dead wife an adulteress casts asper-
sions on all his daughters. In fact, Regan is *not* "glad to see" him.
The vow, therefore, to invade the tomb and divorce their mother
as "adulteress" has force. (A like dilemma dogs Hamlet, who, in
cursing a mother, must curse himself.) If sins are inherited as
Lear's execration implies, his cry a few lines on that Gonerill
is "depraved" tars Regan too. Nor can Cordelia be excluded.
Thwarted love is the argument of the characters in the play—only
two survive their "nature," Albany and Edgar. The reasons for this
will soon be obvious. It is not necessary to take Lear's charge of
adultery against his wife seriously to explain the "nature" of his
daughters. His own character does. Shakespeare is explicit about
this for, in his parallel plot, he makes sure to establish the reason
for the difference in natures between Edmund and Edgar. Edmund's evil disposition—relieved at the last moment by a touch of
good, which only emphasizes this notion of genetic inheritance—
is ascribed by his brother to their father's adultery, the womb of
Edmund's mother, "The dark and vicious place where thee he got"
(*FF.*5.3: 3133). No such argument can be brought against Regan
and Gonerill unless there has been adultery (which would make
Cordelia suspect too). The King himself recognizes this when he
declaims on the heath before the blind Gloucester, "Gloucester['s]
bastard Son was kinder to his Father, / Than my Daughters got
'tween the lawful sheets" (*FF.*4.6: 2560–61). Lear pardons adultery.
What Lear fears is a worse crime. Is it possible though that the
daughters reciprocate his passion for them? Is anger a form of
desire?

The answers to the questions are given by the Fool. They are
addressed in a children's riddle or joke, an ominous one grounded
in the erotic. He or she (for the jester's sexual status is ambivalent)
in speech and persona stands always at the point of metamorphosis, of changing from one person to another. It is an obsessive stage
action for a playwright who understands the power of hallucina-
tion—onstage change—over an audience and its implications. In
King Lear one sees the transformations of Edgar through Poor Tom,
and, through a host of bumpkins, Kent into Caius. (In *Hamlet*, the

major character himself shifts from madman to actor to prince.) The Fool jogs the elbow of King Lear a moment before the meeting at Gloucester's castle that will create the final rupture between Lear and his older daughters. On the slithery tongue of the Fool (and Lear will soon echo his Fool), lust and anger "Change places . . . handy-dandy" (FF. 4.6: 2597). He reveals to the King the nature of his anger, as the latter cries out.

> *Lear.* . . .
> Oh me my heart! My rising heart! But down.
> *Fool.* Cry to it Nuncle; as the Cockney did to the
> Eels, when she put 'em i' th' Paste alive, she knap't 'em
> o'th' coxcombs with a stick, and cried ["]down wantons,
> down;["]³
>
> (FF.2.4: 1397–1401)

Is it only the joke of a foolish pastry cook? The anger is burlesqued in the eel, rising out of the pudding, or paste, like a phallus plunging in the wet womb, alive, erect, to be struck, forced down. Down, however, is inevitably up—up and down, implying both repression of anger and intercourse. This obscene jab of the Fool warns Lear what lies behind his anger—desire.

It is impossible for Lear to repress rage, for its corollary is inadmissible sexual heat. Balked of his daughters' love, the King turns against the world and the universe and tries to crack the mold of humanity by calling for a universal holocaust, the end of seed, creation, sex:

> . . . And thou all-shaking Thunder,
> Strike flat the thick Rotundity o'th' world,
> Crack Nature[']s molds, all germaines spill at once
> That makes ingrateful Man.
>
> (FF.3.2: 1661–64)

It is a night of nakedness that Lear is caught in, lashing back and forth, at the world, at himself. "Things that love night, / Love not such nights as these:" Kent exclaims (FF.3.2: 1694–95). But Lear can not come in out of the "dreadful pudder" until he has stripped away his own concealments. To himself he addresses the cry: "Tremble thou Wretch, / That hast within thee undivulged Crimes / Unwhipped of Justice. Hide thee, thou Bloody hand; / Thou Perjur'd, and thou Simular of Virtue / That art Incestuous, . . ." (3.2: 1704–8). At the end of the soliloquy, he admits to as much, for the "close pent-up guilts" that cry for "grace" are his—threatening a bloody hand, Lear has exiled Kent, and he has perjured his oaths to the gods, dreaming of Cordelia and incest.

> . . . . Close pent-up guilts,
> Rive your concealing Continents, and cry
> These dreadful Summoners' grace. I am a man,
> More sinn'd against, than sinning.
>
> (FF.3.2: 1710–13)

That final, pathetic cry of the naked human being is the King's only plea of justification. His nakedness is his defense. Only after its admission, does he feel his cold. No wonder then that in Poor Tom's nakedness, Lear sees his own. He flashes at Kent who suggests that the madman has no daughter: "Death Traitor, nothing could have subdued / To such a lowness, but his unkind Daughters" (FF.3.4: 1851–52). But if one reads the line carefully, his daughters' unkindness has exposed Lear's flesh, its lust, not simply its physical nakedness. One can not fail to hear the comic in the lines that immediately follow, as Lear asks in all seriousness of the madman, "Is it the fashion, that discarded Fathers, / Should have thus little mercy on their flesh[?]" (FF.3.4: 1853–54). If Pillicock indeed is a pet name for a child, then there is something obscene in this oblique admission of incest in Poor Tom's refrain, a moment later, echoing Lear's "'twas this flesh begot / Those Pelican Daughters," "Pillicock sat on Pillicock Hill, alow: alow, loo, loo!" Whether "Pillicock Hill" is a child's name or not, it is certainly a synonym for the "mount of Venus." Edgar as Poor Tom rocks back and forth to the "alow: alow, loo, loo!" (FF.3.4: 1857) as if sitting on the hill of his mistress.[4] As an erotic reply to Lear's complaint about his daughters, it suggests that Lear look to his own cravings in the flesh. In his inspiration, Edgar as Poor Tom feels Lear's pulse and echoes it. His crime, too, Poor Tom calls, is lust, "the act of darkness" (FF.3.4: 1867). He has been "One, that slept in the / contriving of Lust, and waked to do it" (FF.3.4: 1869–70).

How well Tom's confession catches Lear's drift can be seen in the stage action that follows. On the surface the King's offer of his coat is an act of compassion. Yet from the King's line about Tom's putative daughters, the action in a more literal sense is one of fellowship. Lear begins to strip, to become the "poor, bare, forked Animal." The fool, appalled, protests and strikes even closer to home, to Lear's conscience, "Prithee Nunckle be contented, 'tis a naughty / night to swim in. Now a little fire in a wild Field, / were like an old Lecher's heart, a small spark, all the rest / on's body, cold" (FF.3.4: 1891–94).

* * *

The most difficult role in the play is Edgar's, jumping from innocent to fool and madman. It is rarely given to a leading actor, which
its quick changes and final authority demand. The bland, gullible
Edgar, becomes in his metamorphosis a lewd sexual buffoon. (I
have yet to see this explicit on the stage though the lines make it
apparent.) There is obviously anger in such a transformation, a
playing out of Edgar's revulsion, possible fascination, with the sexual indiscretion of his father. Lear has no sons—Edgar will become
his heir. At the very moment of Lear's chastisement for "an old
Lecher's heart," by his other surrogate child, the Fool, old Gloucester appears. "Look, here comes a walking fire" (FF.3.4: 1894), cries
the Fool, referring to the torch the Earl holds in hand, but also to
the "little fire," of lechery within. In the stage masquerade, in
which nakedness becomes the most effective costume, Edgar, as
Poor Tom, has his moment of revenge. Edgar's revenge is not for
being driven out of the house—that was Edmund's crime, though
its commission is encouraged by Gloucester's underlying anxiety;
his revenge is for his father's adultery whose nervous confession
in a series of jokes is the argument of the opening lines of *King
Lear*. Why displace the King's tragedy with Gloucester's on the
heath, just as the Fool has laid bare the royal conscience? It is because Tom's denunciation of his father's lechery makes the parallel
plot serve as a pointer. Gloucester's sin is obvious; Lear's is not.
The son's denunciation of the father stings Lear and his daughters:

> This is the foul Flibbertigibbet; he begins at
> Curfew, and walks at first Cock: He gives the Web
> and the Pin, squints the eye, and makes the Hare-lip;
> Mildews the white Wheat, and hurts the poor Crea-
> ture of earth.
> > *Swithold* footed thrice the old,
> > He met th Night-Mare, and her nine-fold;
> > Bid her a-light, and her troth-plight,
> > And aroynt thee Witch, aroynt thee.

> (FF.3.4: 1895–1903)

King Lear reeks of the ditch, "The dark and vicious place where
thee he got," as Edgar disparages Edmund's begetting at the end.
The rain that falls in these series of scenes does more than discomfort the characters. It thrusts them into the ditch, the "dark and
vicious place" of the play's center. There is no graver moment in
the plot than that in which Poor Tom gives the whirring descrip-

tion of himself as a creature of ditches, "Curfew . . . Harelip . . . Mildews," like the lecherous child of Mother Goose, little Tom Tittlemouse ("Little Tommy Tittlemouse / lived in a little house / he caught fishes / in other men's ditches."). Edgar listens to himself deprecated by his father's, Gloucester's, laconic (as if it does not touch him) "Hath your Grace no better company?"

Aggrieved, the elder son flashes, "The Prince of Darkness is a Gentleman. *Modo* / he's call'd, and *Mahu*"[5] (*FF*.3.4: 1921–22). Edgar asserts his pedigree as one possessed by the devil. It is not Edgar, however, who has been consort to the "Prince of Darkness," but his father, Gloucester. The repartee is dangerous to Edgar's disguise, for the names of the devil in disguise ring in a way that is almost literary. The question of pedigree—"breeding," to use Gloucester's word when speaking of Edmund's birth in the play's first moments and turning the polite phrase into a coarser farmyard intimation—is very much on the legitimate son's mind, and he can not resist the thrust.

Something in the madman's tone catches Gloucester's ear. Not understanding (for the devil is associated still in his mind with Edgar's purported treachery), still he hears the tone of accusation and snaps back in a remark that returns Tom/Edgar to his own shame and nakedness. "Our flesh and blood, my Lord, is grown so / vile, that it doth hate what gets it" (*FF*.3.4: 1923–24). Edgar shivers, "Poor Tom's acold" (*FF*.3.4: 1925).

A lesser playwright would have left the King content with the counsel of his "good Athenian." The scenes in the rain on the storm drenched heath of act 3 would have been the end of Lear's nakedness, anger, and repentance, the barking of the dogs, "Trey, Blanch, and Sweet-heart." (How resonant that last reference to Cordelia, tear-stained.) Yet anger runs on in King Lear into terror. Lear is met naked on the heath in act 4—naked, not raging, at least in the sense of the storm scenes, but rather, crying out in fear of sex and woman. His ringing lines do not issue out of mistreatment. They reveal a pathology, a self revulsion. The womb of his wife *has* been a "sepulcher," and he has burned in his own incestuous fires. His orgiastic cry, "Let Copulation thrive!" will be answered by a vision of the vagina as a burning hole in the same speech, but not before he has pictured the elder dame of virtue as sweating in sexual desire, "riotous appetite":

Behold yond simpring Dame, whose face between her
Forkes presages Snow; that minces Virtue, & do's shake
the head to hear of pleasures name. The Fitchew, nor

the soiled Horse goes too't with a more riotous appetite. Down from the waist they are Centaurs, though
Women all above: but to the Girdle do the Gods inherit, beneath is all the Fiends. There's hell, there's darke-
ness, there is the sulphurous pit; burning, scalding, stench,
consumption: Fie, fie, fie; pah, pah:

(FF.4.6: 2563–71)

Why this nightmare of the womb as an engulfing horror of judgment that fills Lear's body with such vileness that he has to spit it
out? The juices of lust turn from sweetness into the "paste" spit
from his mouth, "pah, pah . . ."? It is terror of a primal taboo violated. Lear's only sexual sin can be incest. "Adultery" he has just
pardoned.

Lear's speech speaks of "Copulation" in general rather than incest, but its context addresses specific fears. The peroration begins
with the portrait of an aging woman who pretends to a virtue she
does not possess and disguises her "riotous" sexual "appetite."
Finally the soliloquy ends not in an image of copulation but one of
judgment—fear of sex. This answers to an anxiety that exceeds by
far even the "riotous appetite" of an old king who ought to know
better—the anxiety of incest.

King Lear like Hamlet has brutal frankness. Wisdom is abstract in
the play and can not avert the main horror of the action. Wisdom
brings a kind of calm to its possessor, but can not save him. So
Lear goes on with his desire. Its language is no longer that of the
"riotous appetite" of "Centaurs." The attendant enters; the King
wakes up in his dream world, his daughter Cordelia's arms. The
imagery becomes spiritual. "Thou art a Soul in bliss, but I am
bound / Upon a wheel of fire . . . . You are a spirit I know . . ."
(FF. 4.7: 2795–96, 2799). If indeed "the great rage . . . is kill'd in
him" as the attendant reports, and the ethereal has replaced lust
in the King's imagination, the root of selfishness remains. His
underlying wish to possess his daughter is as strong as ever. Is the
fire burned out? Desire to have Cordelia is what directs Lear to a
final, fatal mistake. Taken captive with his daughter a few hours
later, in act 5, scene 2, Lear's blindness leads him to refuse Cordelia's request that the two "see these Daughters, and these Sisters."
The pathos of the moment and the prettiness of the imagery mask
the fact that Lear now imagines he can enjoy what he sought in
the play's first moments, exclusive possession of Cordelia's "kind
nursery." In Cordelia's eyes one sees tears, but, in Lear's voice,
hears almost elation.

No, no, no, no: come, let's away to prison,
We two alone will sing like Birds i'th'Cage:
When thou dost ask me blessing, I'll kneel down
And ask of thee forgiveness: So we'll live,
And pray, and sing, and tell old tales, and laugh
At gilded Butterflies: and hear (poor Rogues)
Talk of Court news, and we'll talk with them too,
Who loses, and who wins; who's in, who's out;
And take upon's the mystery of things,
As if we were Gods spies: And we'll wear out
In a wall'd prison, packs and sects of great ones,
That ebb and flow by th'Moon. . . .

Upon such sacrifices, my *Cordelia*,
The Gods themselves throw Incense.
Have I caught thee?
He that parts us, shall bring a Brand from Heaven,
And fire us hence, like Foxes: wipe thine eyes,
the good years shall devour them, flesh and fell,
Ere they shall make us weep?
We'll see e'm starv'd first; come.

(FF.5.2: 2948–68)

"Birds in the cage," is not only ominous, of which Lear in his haste to cajole Cordelia does not seem aware, but also recalls his earlier line, "the Wren goes to't!" The lappings of the moon, the "mystery of things," and the notion that "We two alone" will be "Gods spies," deliberately mystify, etherealize the scene. Does Lear believe (as he declares) that all Gonerill and Regan wish to do to him and Cordelia is "make us weep?" He would indeed be "child-changed" as Cordelia observed earlier (*FF*.4.7: 2766). It *is* true and signifies that he is as blind with love in act 5, as in act 1. What Lear wants, he gets—Cordelia's tears: "Have I caught thee?" (As captive bird, fluttering, a grim image!) Having gotten them, he cautions her not to cry in front of her sisters. No, their feelings shall only be for each other. "We two alone . . . ," and then a few moments later, "Upon such sacrifices, my *Cordelia*, / The Gods themselves throw Incense." But the image of the gods strewing incense smacks more of the bed than the altar. (The King is speaking of himself as priest and his daughter as vestal virgin. This temple in its sexual associations also recalls Iphiginia and Agamemnon, a sacrifice that ecapsulates the tragedy of the Trojan War in the murder of a daughter by a father; the revenge of the mother in turn upon the murderous father.) Lear has forgotten his daughter's remonstrance in the first act: "Why have my Sisters

Husbands, if they say / They love you all? Happily when I shall wed / That Lord, whose hand must take my plight, shall carry / Half my love with him, half my Care, and Duty, / Sure I shall never marry like my sisters" (FF.1.1. 106–10). France is not dead, although his willingness to let his impulsive wife cross the channel (without him in the Folio) gives pause. Can he control her? Cordelia's silence before Lear's assurance of mutual self-sufficiency is unsettling. One can argue that she does not wish to contradict the fallen defeated old man. Equally one might say that she acquiesces in a dream of confinement as a form of "souls in bliss."

In the last sight of Lear, Shakespeare chooses to suggest the unmentionable. Far from being frail, broken, the King enters bearing the body of his child. He boasts of having killed the fierce captain who was hanging her. The rage flickers in that last moment. He cries out on death and lets us know that his surrogate child, the Fool, is hanged too.

Now the King bends to a task beyond his strength. Again the stage interpreters have falsely imagined a man, exhausted, on the verge of heart failure. They are misled by two of the stage onlookers—Albany and Kent, both tired men. (Note that the younger man, Edgar, does not share their attitude.) Albany, obtuse as always, can not hear the sense of Lear's lines or understand his fixed idea that makes him indifferent to both the introductions and information of events, buzzing over his head. Kent, whose understanding does not penetrate beyond the wheel of Fortune, can not appreciate the "wheel of fire" Lear is bound upon. "He hates him, / That would upon the rack of this tough world / Stretch him out longer" (FF.5.3: 3287–89), the world weary Duke exclaims.

It is not so. Lear has stated what wheel he is bound to, both in this world and the world to come. His terror, but also his dream of mastery, extends to that other world, the hellish universe: " . . . I am bound / Upon a wheel of fire, that mine own tears / Do scal'd, like molten Lead" (FF.4.7: 2795–97). In the last moment, he summons superhuman prodigious strength, straining so that the top button of his cloak catches tight against his throat, breaking his heart. He answers his own "Thou'lt come no more, / Never, never, never, never, never" (FF.5.3: 3279–80) with the vision of Cordelia as a spirit in the other world, rising. Olivier's Lear sinks down on Cordelia's breast in an incestuous last embrace. I would set this possibility aside. In fact, Shakespeare seems to have left a clear description of how Lear's death should be staged. In the parallel plot, he has Edgar give the details of how Gloucester looked in the last moment of life: "his flawed heart / (Alack too weak the conflict to support) / Twixt two extremes of passion, joy and grief, / Burst smilingly" [FF.5.3: 3159–62].[6] Again if the Folio is Shakespeare's final word, a comparison is instructive. The three "nevers" of the Quarto are increased to five.[7] The elongated agony "O" of the Quarto Lear's last word, an exclamation, "O thou wilt / come no more, never, never, never. Pray you undo this button, / thank you sir. O, o, o, o, o," become (additions in boldface):

> Thoult come no more,
> Never, never, never, **never, never.**
> Pray you undo this Button. Thank you Sir,
> **Do you see this, look on her? Look her lips,**
> **Look there, look there.** *He dies.*
>
> (FF.5.3: 3279–83)

Lear is rising, his daughter in his arms, rising toward a spiritual not a bodily life where the communion, intercourse, of father and daughter is perfect. Does he expires with his lips against hers? Or is he trying to uplift them both? Yet by way of paradox, what he is striving with is her spirit, to bring her back into this world from the other, to breathe life into the body. He dies in the supreme effort to raise the dead—and one is never sure whether he feels her for an instant coming back to life, or sees her spirit, which he hastes to join. He is between worlds at the last moment of the play, a looming specter—not just larger than life, beyond life—and we are left behind. The fall of his body onto the stage, tangled with Cordelia's, leaves us alone. There is no adequate response. The bodies are borne off together, Kent trailing them, the frustrated lover of both father and daughter unable to imagine a life without their presence, the tension of attraction and fear to which he has been priest.

That moment of hideous magic lingers in Lear's final lines—the illusion of Cordelia's breath, brought back from the dead. Did it happen? "Look on her? Look her lips, / Look there, look there." Lear's laughter in death fills the stage—and so the riddle of Kent's, "I have a journey, Sir, shortly to go / My Master calls me: I must not say no." There is no single God, "master," in the world of *King Lear*. The deities are multiple. It is Lear who is calling Kent out of the world, haunting the stage, in the form of the druidic presence that the King's bearing threatened from the first. In this tenor one must hear Edgar's lines, concluding the play in the Folio (the speech is Albany's in the Quarto) not as a statement of the general exhaustion, but as a conundrum of Poor Tom: "We that are young, / Shall never see so much, nor live so long" (*FF*.5.3: 3300–1). What have they seen? It is not the tragedy but the mystery that lies somehow beyond their grasp—and ours—now and forever in the fullness of human years.

Shakespeare has left the confession of the father who wishes to take his children in the flesh. The last shadow of King Lear is the first of Hamlet, the threat of possession even unto death.

3

The Itch Revises

Iꜰ William Shakespeare had rethought the *King Lear* of 1605–1606—the "Quarto"—it was in a relatively short span of years, for Shakespeare would retire from the stage some seven years later and die in 1616. How and why did that confession of the flesh alter as time made the playwright feel his own resignation of powers coming on? Shakespeare's revision to the first scene in the Folio is telling (in boldface below). It falls in the lines in which Lear extends himself to his daughters.

> . . . tell me my daughters,
> Which of you shall we say doth love us most,
> That we our largest bounty may extend,
> Where merit doth most challenge it,
> *Gonorill,* our eldest borne, speak first?

(Q.1.1.45–49)

> . . . Tell me my daughters
> **(Since now we shall divest us both of Rule,**
> **Interest of Territory, Cares of State)**
> Which of you shall we say doth love us most,
> That we, our largest bounty may extend
> Where **Nature** doth **with** merit challenge. *Gonerill,*
> Our eldest borne, speak first.

(F.F.1.1.53–59)

In the Quarto, Lear's question is blunt, going right to the division of the kingdom, "Which of you shall we say doth love us most." In the Folio, he dallies over the question, "(Since we shall divest us both of Rule, / Interest of Territory, Cares of State)." It is an aside, and, if the actor punctuates it so, the words speak of the King's vulnerability, his appeal. The audience must feel the pinch of the inevitable, the playwright's advancing years dogging his footsteps. It might be Prospero, resigning his powers. The Quarto wants speech only to confirm deeds, what must be obvious, and

so King Lear's purpose is simply stated; "That we our largest bounty may extend, / Where merit doth most challenge it." In the Folio, the King's desire to probe the recesses of the daughters, their intentions and privacy, is expressed, "That we, our largest bounty may extend / Where *Nature* doth *with* merit challenge." It is the "nature" of the tie between daughter and father that the Folio's Lear wants to know, a dangerous wish. Again, in the lines to Cordelia, the older playwright rather than hurrying to the baiting of Cordelia, delays. The King no longer sums up Cordelia's position as he does in the Quarto:

> . . . but now our joy,
> Although the last, not least in our dear love,
> What can you say to win a third, more opulent
> Than your sisters.[?]
>
> (Q.1.1.74–77)

Shakespeare, in the Folio, turns his former line on its head. Cordelia is not introduced with a "but" following Gonerill. Coming to a full stop, after awarding a third to Regan and mentioning Gonerill's, the King begins with:

> . . . Now our Joy,
> Although our last and least; to whose young love,
> The Vines of France, and Milk of Burgundy,
> Strive to be interest. What can you say, to draw
> A third, more opulent the[a]n your Sisters? speak.
>
> (FF.1.1.88–92)

Cordelia is indeed her father's "last," but she has gone through a significant metamorphosis between Quarto and Folio. In the former, the King admitted she was far from being the "least" in his affection, which was a prologue to her presumably getting the lion's share of the kingdom, although married to a potential enemy of England, the king of France. In the Folio, Cordelia becomes not just the youngest, but, as the conjunction "and" emphasizes, she *is* also the "least." The meaning of the last term is ambiguous. Does it simply repeat the earlier "last" in the sense of the youngest, or does it now emphasize her inferior position, which would presumably draw a smaller portion? The word "least" preceded by "and" emphasizes her vulnerability, which is parallel to the King's own as in the lines added about his divestiture. The Folio's contrast is not between "last" and "least" but between "joy" and "last and least." Suddenly in a scene in which the King will be appealing above all for love from his daughters, Shakespeare has inserted the pointer "to whose young love" and the King's rivals for it, France and Burgundy, as if disclaiming Lear's erotic claims on it. The King is teasing, and, of course, so is the playwright, more aware of the danger that his old king is courting.

The "weight" of this teasing on Cordelia is given voice in the shift of adjectives in her aside during the interview of her sister Regan: "Then poor *Cord.* & yet not so, since I am sure / My love['s] more **richer** then my tongue" (*Q.*1.1.69–70). Shakespeare's change in the Folio to " . . . my love's / More **ponderous** than my tongue" (*FF.*1.1.83–84) speaks to the riddling, unstated "nature" of love, in particular the love between father and daughter. It hangs in the air now with the freight of sexual implications, suggesting perhaps the bosom of the young girl, "ponderous" more ominous than the conventional "rich."

Of course the immediate sense of "ponderous" is that Cordelia's love is too weighty to be spoken. This enforces the threat of the first aside after Gonerill's words, that Cordelia's love will fulfill her sister's vaunt and make "speech unable." The specter of comedy haunts the sisters' speeches and their father's reaction. King Lear should burst into open laughter after the first or second "Nothing," of his daughter; it is *too* outrageous, *too* ridiculous. How can she bait him when it is obvious what he is about to do—to dower her more handsomely than the two daughters whose sentiments he rightly suspects? The court too must join in the laughter. It is a burlesque, a daring but successful defiance of her father. This is what the Folio sketches in its additions. (That "nothing" in the exchange between Hamlet and Ophelia refers to "vagina" is something to "ponder" here.[1]) It is only when the defiance, Cordelia's "nothing" goes on, after the joke ought to be over, that the King begins to realize he is not being played with, but being rebuked both for arranging the game and for the sexual claims his game implies. "According to my bond, no more nor less" (*FF.*1.1.99) is where Lear's game is lost. It is this whisper of the truth so unbearable to the King that drives him into a frenzy. At once his sincerity, his mastery, and his potency are called into question. The Folio's cut after the final line, "Sure I shall never marry like my Sisters" (*FF.*1.1.110), is telling. It is redundant to add as the Quarto does, "to love my father all," since Cordelia has already cried, "Why have my Sisters Husbands, if they say / They love you all?" The Folio abbreviation suggests as well that King Lear interrupts because he feels the threat of something even more rash from his daughter's mouth about that "bond," an accusation that he can not face. He begs her to be "tender," the force of his last appeal, "So young, and so untender?" Interruptions, the critic warns, are signs of danger in the drama.[2]

This, however, is to move ahead of the text, or at least ahead of the lines. To understand the climax of the Folio's changes, in which the motive is drawn more clearly to Lear's explosion of rage, "Thy truth then be thy dower," it is necessary to go step by step from the first silence, or refusal, of Cordelia, laying out Shakespeare's revision of the Quarto's dialogue.

> *Lear.* . . . but now our joy,
> Although the last, not least in our dear love,
> What can you say to win a third, more opulent
> Than your sisters.[?]
> *Cord.* Nothing my Lord.
> *Lear.* How, nothing can come of nothing, speak again.
> *Cord.* Unhappy that I am, I cannot heave my heart into my
> mouth, I love your Majesty according to my bond, nor more nor
> less.
> *Lear.* Go to, go to, mend your speech a little,
> Lest it may mar your fortunes.
>
> (*Q*.1.1.74–84)

> *Lear.* . . . . Now our Joy,
> Although **our** last **and** least; **to whose young** love,
> **The Vines of France, and Milk of Burgundy,**
> **Strive to be interest.** What can you say, to **draw**
> A third, more opulent the[a]n your Sisters? **speak.**
> *Cor.* Nothing my Lord.
> *Lear.* **Nothing?**
> *Cor.* **Nothing.**
> *Lear.* Nothing **will** come of nothing, speak again.
> *Cor.* Unhappy that I am, I cannot heave
> My heart into my mouth: I love your Majesty
> According to my bond, **no** more nor less.
> *Lear.* **How, how, Cordelia?** mend your speech a little,
> Lest **you** may mar your Fortunes.
>
> (*FF.*1.1.88–101)

The climax of these changes comes on the exchange of "nothings." Shakespeare, in the Folio, delays, draws out, makes almost comic, this exchange, repeats the word "nothing" so as to make one experience the agonized frustration of the father who can get no verbal satisfaction from his "Joy . . . last and least" in spite of his confession of helplessness. There are five *spoken* "nothings" in the Folio as against three in the Quarto. A sixth "nothing" is implied in the pause that the actor playing Lear, sensitive to Shakespeare's change of nuance in the Folio, will insert between, "What can you say, to draw / a Third, more opulent then your Sisters?" (punctuated in the Folio by a question mark) and the silence implicit in Lear's command or cajolement in the same line after a "ponderous" caesura to "speak." For the first part of the plea that, in the Quarto, drew Cordelia's "Nothing"; in the Folio, evokes no spoken response. It is followed, however, by Lear's cry, "Speak!" Cordelia's refusal to speak anything is only a punctuated "nothing!" The public teasing or humiliation of the fond father, an old king, by his youngest child is being dramatized. Is Cordelia stubborn, or is she treating Lear to a round in his own game? It is *deliberately not* clear. The King himself can easily burst into laughter as the shaggy dog joke goes on.

There may be another two "silent nothings," from Cordelia, earlier on. One comes if the King pauses after "What can you say?" challenging his youngest to outdo the extravagant words of her elders. Then, in the face of her silence, like a bluff in a game of cards, Lear encourages Cordelia with, "to draw / A third," which met by her silence (*another* possible "nothing") *draws* from him, his secret, "more opulent than your sisters?" Here indeed the court might gasp, since the question, debated in the very first lines of the play, "the division of the Kingdom," is now given a new twist. The court watching the smile on the King's face grow even broader, after his "speak!" (since Cordelia has tricked him into revealing his intention without saying a word), listens with shock as she seems to bluff once more with her answer, "Nothing." One hears the King break into loud and nervous laughter in which everyone else joins, as Lear repeats Cordelia's word, "Nothing?" Again there is a long, nervous pause, into which the King, shaking off his laughter, mutters, still amused but sarcastic, "Nothing will come of nothing, speak again." Or he may make the first half as a joke, "Nothing will come of nothing," to the appreciative roars of the court. His court as is shortly learned, can "show . . . like a riotous Inn." Into this merriment, he might well let himself *plead* again, "speak again." In motivating the action, it is not through words but through awkward silences to which Cordelia subjects Lear that the action builds to its catastrophic, almost comic, climax.

The reply of Cordelia that stops the game, the "play" of "nothing" but not of words, starts with a play on the aside that Lear can not have heard. Her love is "ponderous," and, therefore, she can not "heave / My heart into my mouth." The Quarto misses this irony, but the game between them would end in the same passage in the explosive force of the word "bond," which reminds him of their relationship as father and daughter, only what is "right fit" as she will remark in a moment, "*no more,*" even though it is softened by, "*nor* less." (Notice how much stronger this is than the Quarto's "nor more, nor / less.)

It is in the Folio's "How," possibly followed by a long pause of the King's before his second, "how," that the atmosphere changes. Again the Folio points this, as the King refers not to the speech, "*it* may mar your fortunes" (*Q.*), but his daughter: "*you* may mar your Fortunes" (*FF.*). Cordelia does not "mend" her speech, oblivious it would seem of her "Fortunes." She hammers at Lear with the *b* of her previous reference to their *bond*: "You have *begot* me, *bred* me, loved me / I return those duties *back* as are right fit, *Obey* you . . . ." The last is the very opposite it would seem of the language of love. She throws his affection, it must seem to the King, back in his face, and, in the Folio, this is stressed by not three, but five spoken "nothings," and any number of unspoken ones. It is Cordelia's rejection of her father's implicit demand for an all-consuming love, to which her sisters hypocritically seem to acquiesce, as if their husbands meant nothing to them, "Sure I shall never marry like my sisters." The Quarto adds the barbed reference to a love that must be incestuous, "to love my father all." It is hurled in King Lear's teeth as a question: "All? What do you want from me, your daughter?"

The Quarto's repetition of "all," as I remarked earlier, is redundant. The actress, who, with eyes flashing and bosom heaving, searches Lear's eyes for a response to "all," will see the spark that the Folio ignites in the briefer but pointed reference to the sisters' "right fit," or "legitimate" ("fine word" as Edmund points out) sexual bonds. Subsequent events in the play make clear why Cordelia's reference to her sisters is disparaging. Cordelia understands them, and Lear will soon grope towards understanding, speaking of it in his general denunciation of women and the vagina, "but to the Girdle do the Gods, inhe-/ rit, beneath is all the Fiends. There's hell, there's dark- / ness," (*FF.*4.6:2568–70). The briefer, sharper "Why have my Sisters Husbands?" of the Folio questions the manhood of the dukes. The King ignores, however, the "truth" that Cordelia has spoken. He is already lost in self-pity, his fantasy broken in on. That fantasy will be spoken to again, in a revelation characteristic of the Folio's addition (boldfaced below).

. . . . The barbarous *Scythian,*
Or he that makes his generation messes
To gorge his appetite, shall **to my bosom**
Be as well neighbor'd, pitied, and reliev'd,
As thou my sometime Daughter.

(FF.1.1.123–27)

"My bosom" the addition of the Folio, suggests the child sucking on the Father/Mother's tit, an indicator of the King's ambivalent Eros with his daughter. This also touches the mysterious, dead mother—a mother alluded to viciously, in the King's outcry on Gonerill, "Degenerate Bastard" (*FF*.1.4: 764) and again in act 2, scene 4 when King Lear threatens Regan for a loving welcome: "if thou should'st not be glad, / I would divorce me from thy Mother Tomb, / Sepulchering an Adulteress" (*FF*.2.4: 1408–10). Lear's "bosom" also suggests a possible sexual tie as in Regan's remark, "I know you are of her bosom" (*FF*.4.5: 2413), to Gonerill's steward. In the Quarto, although the lines are cut from the Folio, the language in which Regan accuses Edmund of finding her "brothers way, / To the forefended place," i.e., sleeping with Gonerill, uses the "bosom" in parallel to the more abstract, though absolutely specific, "conjunct," " . . . you have been conjunct and bo- / som'd with her" (*Q*.5.1: 2587–88).

Overarching the particulars of the quarrel between father and daughter in the play is the question of the King's desire to retreat into his fantasy of retirement. Kent in the Folio objects not only to the judgment on Cordelia but to the splitting of the kingdom. "Reserve thy state" (*FF*.1.1.159) he cries, not "Reverse thy doom" (*Q*.1.1.141) as in the Quarto, and again, "revoke thy **gift**" (*FF*.1.1.178), not "Revoke thy doom" (*Q*.1.1.158). In the Quarto, Kent gives the King's withdrawal of affection or "Friendship" (*Q*.1.1.174) as his reason for preferring to go into exile. In the Folio, Lear's retreat into fantasies, which turns the court into a tyranny, forces Kent's departure. Not "Friendship lives hence" but "**Freedom** lives hence" (*FF*.1.1.195), for the latter, a more appropriate and biting antonym to "banishment."

"Friendship," the Quarto's word, is too pale for the Folio's understanding of Kent's quarrel. All through the later text, references to the deeper struggles of the play are strengthened. Cordelia's apostrophe to her sisters on leaving them is, thus, more ominous, not the earlier version's "use well our Father" (*Q*.1.1.267), but "**Love** well our Father" (*FF*.1.1.296). The sexual underlies two violent and irrational disruptions of the believable that are the engines of the play: Lear's turning on his most loving daughter, Cordelia, and the Earl of Gloucester's turning on his "legitimate" son. In the subplot as well, Shakespeare increases sexual tension in his Folio changes. After the revisions in the exchange between Lear and Cordelia, where Shakespeare tried to make his scene more believable, the second major Folio alteration, not surprisingly, touches the playwright's nervousness about the motivation in the subplot. A number of lines are added or cut in the scene in which Gloucester is led by Edmund to believe that Edgar is plotting to usurp the earldom. The Bastard imagines his father's legitimate marriage as "a dull stale tired bed" (*FF*.1.2: 347), which has created the "fop," his brother, Edgar. The "nature" then of the sexual act determines the character of the child begot. Nature is seen as both cosmic and personal, although Edmund mocks the former, "nature," as revealed in the stars. Edmund worships "nature," as his "Goddess" (*FF*.1.2: 335), but it is nature in its "lusty stealth" that he adores. The link between the nature of the stars and the personal nature of the sexual act is something both son and father deny. For the earl of Gloucester, "nature" is at fault; nature is departing from its "legitimate" course. Gloucester's belief, however, makes him credulous, just as Edmund's makes him cynical. The Earl, still blinded by Nature's "lusty stealth," can not see the "bias of Nature," nor distinguish the son on whom the stars' prediction falls. The Earl of Gloucester's additional lines in the Folio address his prophetic if misguided horror;

> . . . . This villain of mine comes under the
> prediction; there's Son against Father, the King falls from
> bias of Nature, there's Father against Child. We have
> seen the best of our time. Machinations, hollowness,
> treachery, and all ruinous disorders follow us disquietly
> to our Graves"
>
> (*FF*.1.2: 439–44)

The lines speak to a terror that Gloucester's crude joke about Edmund's begetting in the very first scene belied. "There was good sport at his making," took all of Kent's tact to deflect. The line is echoed with anger at the end of the play by Edgar's answer both to his father's jest and his brother's mocking defense of adultery: "The dark and vicious place where thee he got, / Cost him his eyes" (*FF*.5.3: 3133–34). Edgar's victory refutes both Edmund's vision of a universe whose heavens are empty and powerless and of a nature who stamps her offspring according to the anarchic power of desire. Edmund's defeat in arms belies his claim that bastards

> . . . in the lusty stealth of Nature, take
> More composition, and fierce quality,
> Then doth within a dull stale tired bed
> Go to th' creating a whole tribe of Fops
> Got 'tween a sleep, and wake?

(FF.1.2: 345–49)

Edmund is twisting terms, calling his shape "true" rather than his mind, his mind "generous," which seems in his lexicon to mean "grasping." The word "honest" spoken with contempt of his "legitimate" brother's mother, "honest Madams issue" breathes mockingly, obscenely in its apposition of "Madams" with "honest."[3] There is, though, some truth to Edmund's observation. The play is about "the lusty stealth of Nature." It is their secret lives, their hidden natures, that overwhelm Lear and Gloucester and make them vulnerable to sudden irrational terror. Lear's sin remains covered, secret; Gloucester's past is brought to light. Shakespeare, however, sees both King and Earl as victims not just of their "natures" but also of Nature itself. Edmund speaks to this when he talks of its "lusty stealth," and Lear when he hears Nature's molds for human beings breaking up in the thunder and lightning on the heath. Why was the cry about "hollowness, / treachery, and all ruinous disorders" that "follow us disquietly / to our Graves" added in the Folio since Shakespeare seems to have been revising toward swifter action, clarity, and rubbing out redundancy?

The Folio additions do not speak only to the playwright's further questions about the Earl's unnatural or "natural" behavior; Shakespeare is also struggling with one of the most difficult actions to play in *King Lear*, Gloucester's inexplicable surrender to suspicion on the basis of a letter rather than an encounter with Edgar. The turning against a beloved child is of course parallel to the King's action, but the latter's is staged. Gloucester has to be seen as "ripe" to crack. He is not in his dotage, but, beset by fears of "Machinations," he is too old to be effectual. Just a bit tiresome, silly, sharing with Polonius a certain lecherous streak, Gloucester's act of loyalty to the King still ennobles him. Then the truth that he learns in the moment of his most extreme torture brings him, like Ophelia, to the act of suicide. This is a difficult moment for an actor to make convincing because Gloucester remains too sane to embrace suicide. He needs Ophelia's madness, but that is reserved to King Lear. In Gloucester, the will to suicide, like extreme suspicion, is momentary, provoked by depression, which operates like hysteria upon the character. The Folio's additions are to give Gloucester the superstitious dread to embrace Edmund's suggestions. Adding to the credulous father, however, Shakespeare cuts from the incredulous son. Why isn't Edgar more suspicious of his brother? Lines about "prediction" are taken away from Edmund in the Folio for they serve no purpose. Edgar openly mocks Edmund's busying himself with "prediction," and the latter quickly drops a tack that, in the Quarto, he goes on a few lines with, speaking of "death, dearth, dissolutions of ancient amities, disunions in state, menaces, and maledictions . . . ." Edgar has no patience with such anxiety. Here is the earlier Quarto version:

> *Enter Edgar.*
> *Edgar;* and out he comes like the Catastrophe of the old Co medy, mine is villainous melancholy, with a sigh like them of Bedlam; O these eclipses do portend these divisions.
>
> *Edgar.* How now brother *Edmund*, what serious contemplation are you in?
>
> *Bast.* I am thinking brother of a prediction I read this other day, what should follow these Eclipses.
>
> *Edg.* Do you busy your self about that?
>
> *Bast.* I promise you the effects he writ of, succeed unhappily, as of unnaturalness between the child and the parent, death, dearth, dissolutions of ancient amities, divisions in state, menaces and maledictions against King and nobles, needles diffidences, banishment of friends, dissipation of Cohorts, nuptial breaches, and I know not what.
>
> *Edg.* How long have you been a sectary Astronomical?
>
> *Bast.* Come, come, when saw you my father last?
>
> (Q.1.2: 412–27)

Shakespeare must have realized that Edmund's echo of his father's anxiety falling on deaf ears and only provoking Edgar's ironic "How long have you been a sectary Astronomical" made it that much more difficult for the audience to accept Edgar's faith in his brother, Edmund's, anxiety about the threat to Edgar's life. The

Folio cuts to that threat after Edgar's first jibe, "Do you busy your-self with that?"

> *Enter Edgar.*
> Pat; he comes like the Catastrophe of the old Comedy:
> my Cue is villianous Melancholy, with a sigh like *Tom
> o'Bedlam*[4]—O these Eclipses do portend these divi-
> sions. Fa, Sol, La, Me.
>
> *Edg.* How now, Brother *Edmund,* what serious con-
> templation are you in?
>
> *Bast.* I am thinking Brother of a prediction I read this
> other day, what should follow these Eclipses.
>
> *Edg.* Do you busy yourself with that?
>
> *Bast.* I promise you, the effects he writes of succeed
> unhappily.
> When saw you my Father last?
>
> (*FF.*1.2: 462–74)

The condescension of "Come, come," which is necessary for Ed-mund to assert control over Edgar, but difficult to accept, can be cut. Edmund, moreover, is given the musical scale to intone, as if to hint at some sadness that is unspeakable, for the less said, the more suggested. Other cuts are made to quicken the taking of the bait. Edmund's response to Gloucester's exclamation, "He cannot be such a monster," "*Bast.* Nor is not sure," as well as Gloucester's further cry, "To his father, that so tenderly and entirely loves him, heaven and earth!" (*Q.*1,2: 383–86) are deleted in the Folio. The lines of the Earl are bathos, hard for an actor to manage with any convincing show of emotion since Gloucester's reaction is suspi-cion. The action is moving too fast for reflection. There is some-thing too easy about this game, and Edmund's teasing response, "Nor is not sure," does not make it less so.

Shakespeare's uneasiness in these stage games, his revisions, are the dowsing rod's descent to his preoccupation. It is "Nature" which is perverse. "Nature" and its irrational course are "dark and vicious," the "below"; and Gloucester, who, like Lear, has fallen from the "bias of Nature," can not yet face his own complicity.

"The Gods are just" (*FF.*5.3: 3131) Edgar pronounces just before he remarks with some cruelty, even priggishness, "The dark and vicious place where thee he got, / Cost him his eyes." As critics have observed, however, the gods do not seem "just" in *King Lear*, and Edgar is prone when he has put off the persona of Poor Tom to moral epigrams. Edgar's father, the Earl, has wryly undercut his "Ripeness is all," so now the audience remembers Gloucester's "As Flies to wanton Boys, are we to th'Gods, / They kill us for their sport" (*FF*.4.1: 2221–22). Edgar's abstract moralizing is cut away by the Folio, in particular the long speech that begins, "When we our betters see bearing our woes: we scarcely / think, our miseries, our foes" (*Q*.3.6: 1793–1806).[5] One wonders, however, if Edgar does not fall under Regan's biting and true sarcasm about her father; "he hath ever but / slenderly known himself" (*FF*.1.1.318–19). Edgar, after all, in revealing himself may have killed his father. If not a fop, as Edmund hints, when first Edgar is seen, he is certainly an innocent—an innocent, however, chosing a secret self to play, who dramatizes on the stage sexual appetite. Edgar as Tom not only harps on the "dark and vicious place," but also goes through the motions of copulation. Edgar's uninhibited acting out of sexual desire, bounds far beyond the limits of what is permissible for the Fool, who after all despite his shock is a creature of the court, not of the field and ditch outside.

Edgar enacts sexual madness in front of Lear, thrusting up and down in a parody of the sexual act, "Pillicock sat on Pillicock hill, alow: alow, loo, loo" (*FF*.3.4: 1857). This is orgasm on stage (and should be played as such). In this wild flailing Tom of Bedlam, the audience sees the image of a man *in Lear's eyes* who has also been thrust out by his daughters: "slept in the contriving of Lust, and wak'd to do it." (*FF*.3.4: 1869–70). Lear's benediction or insistence *about* Poor Tom is that "nothing could have subdu'd Nature / To such a lowness, but his unkind Daughters. / Is it the fashion, that discarded Fathers, / Should have thus little mercy on their flesh" (*FF*.3.4: 1851–54). These lines echo as Poor Tom admits to harboring unquenchable lust. In this both King Lear and Edgar reflect obliquely the latter's line, "to course his own shadow for a Traitor" (*FF*.3.4: 1838). The irony here, rarely seen on the stage, is that the shadow of good Edgar is the raging demon in the Gloucester blood, recalling the father's salacious reference to the begetting of his bastard, "good sport at his making" (*FF*.1.1.26). The implication of a monster of desire in Edgar struts on the stage, as he boasts about his prowess as an engine of copulation. Not only is he a lad who "serv'd the Lust / of my Mistress heart, and did the act of darkness with / her" (*FF*.3.4: 1866–68), but also his reputation has in his imagination spread to the neighborhood and beyond, because, he has now, "in Women, out-Paramour'd / the Turk" (*FF*.3.4:

1871–72). It is in this context that Lear hears from his Fool, the truth about old men's passion: "Now a little fire in a wild Field, / were like an old Lechers heart, a small spark, all the rest / on's body, cold" (*FF*.3.4: 1892–94).

The Folio insists on laughter—"'tis a naughty / night to swim in" (*FF*.3.4: 1891–92)—laughter for King Lear and his daughter, laughter for Edgar, the "legitimate." Even Gloucester's final line should be preceded with laughter breaking into tears—tears into laughter, the whole of it dismissed with the ambiguous mocking addition of the Folio, "And that's true too" (*FF*.5.2: 2936). The laughter with which Lear greets Cordelia's "nothing," is the laughter that he echoes—mocks, as if he is being fooled, by her again, in his very last breath. It is awful, too awful perhaps to look upon.

4

Hamlet's Father

Wₕₐₜ weighs one down when seeing or reading *Hamlet* is the force of despair, horror, from without—beyond, below the stage. A young man, committed to rational discourse, nevertheless finds himself the prey of the irrational. *King Lear* and *Hamlet* have a common theme—the displacement of a king and father. They are plays written out of the guilt and fear of the child. To detect Shakespeare under the masks of the actors in these plays is difficult precisely because the playwright intended it to be so.[1] The anger against a father can be open in *King Lear* because it is after all, daughters, not sons, who rebel—and three persons instead of one. The baffles in *Hamlet* are far more elaborate since the author's hero, the Prince, shadows him.

In *Hamlet*, two sons are driven mad, murdered on stage. In *Lear*, only Edmund receives this punishment before our eyes, and it is at a brother's not a father's hand. No father in *Hamlet*, not Polonius, Claudius, nor the Ghost, engages our sympathies as does Lear, or even Gloucester. Claudius with his veneer of calm reason and the Ghost with his horrible tale ask sympathy, but the advice of the first is smug, masking fear of discovery, while the rage of the Ghost is finally selfish, callous to the danger he calls his son into. In both cases, the direct audience, the Prince, by his unconventional reaction signals to us, the secondary audience, that something in the delivery of the words is amiss, calling the speaker's sincerity into question. One of *Hamlet*'s most astute critics, notices this: "Claudius, in his opening address to the Council, establishes himself as a practiced exponent of stately double-talk. With unctuous skill, he manages a transition from the old King's death to himself and his inherited queen. Antithesis is condensed into oxymoron: 'delight and dole,' 'defeated joy.' . . . Claudius is virtually winking, when he speaks of 'an auspicious and a dropping eye.'"[2] Hamlet, echoing this rhetoric and its hypocrisy, "ironically . . . sums up the paradoxical situation:

. . . The Funeral bakt-meats
Did coldly furnish forth the Marriage Tables

(FF.1.2.368–69)

The old king, however, the father of Hamlet, also provokes his son's suspicions. The epithet "old Mole" undercuts the Ghost's Senecan rhetoric of horror in a way that is uncomfortably close to Hamlet's treatment of his uncle. (Note that in speaking a few lines before of Claudius and Danish character, the Prince in the Second Quarto, mentions a "vicious mole" [Q2.D: 1.4. 24].) Polonius is the object of Shakespeare's satire on fathers from his first step on stage, a buffoon, "eyes purging thick Amber, or Plum-Tree / gum" (FF.2.2: 1236–37).

From its inception, then, the drama's naked concerns threaten to disclose themselves. *Hamlet* pretends to be a tragedy of revenge based on the murder of the old king, Hamlet, by his brother, Claudius. This *is* the ostensible play, but as a play it is unsatisfactory, breaks down, and is simply out of balance. *Hamlet* goes on and on, and the revenge play ought to have been over hours after we are still held,[3] fascinated by the drama unfolding. It is not the killing of Claudius to which we attend, but that of Hamlet. We are not sure, as the event comes, whether it has been willed, is an accident, or is suicide. While his delay appears to tar Hamlet with the charge of indecision, Shakespeare's drama is careful never to allow the Prince a clear "shot" at Claudius. Hamlet charges himself with tarrying at the beginning: that is sign of his self-awareness, honesty. Shakespeare carefully avoids throughout a situation in which the dramatic events would judge the Prince irrevocably as indecisive. What the author does do, however, is to make his hero so scrupulous about the proof or "grounds" for revenge—and the place and time of execution—as to bring the very notion of revenge outside a court into question. One must note that, at the very end, Hamlet does prove, in front of a literal "court," through actual testimony and evidence, the guilt of Claudius. This is hardly a happy accident. The whole of the play has been tending to such an event. But the delay would be a didactic device if this was its only object. The delay, however, is a symptom of a deep malaise in the playwright who can not let his Prince act until he has resolved his own questions. T. S. Eliot complained that "*Hamlet* . . . is full of some stuff that the writer could not drag to light, contemplate, or manipulate into art. . . . Shakespeare tackled a problem which proved too much for him. Why he attempted it at all is an insoluble puzzle; under compulsion of what experience he attempted to express the inexpressibly horrible, we cannot ever know."[4] While sensitive to the eerie displacement of Shakespeare in *Hamlet*, Eliot begged the question (twitting us by holding *Coriolanus* to be the superior play).

In *Hamlet* anger against the father is concealed in Hamlet's delay. The procrastination of the Prince *might* be justified by conscience—but the moments of mockery and fear give away the presence of other concerns, underlying his actions, his manner of speech.

The incestuous poles of *Hamlet* have been ingeniously kept from public view by Shakespeare. By introducing the attraction of the Prince for his young mother, the design of the old king, Hamlet, on his son's life and flesh is masqueraded. Whereas *King Lear* is entirely a naturalistic play, despite the King's invocation of demon, pagan god, and planet to effect his purposes (none do in fact appear), *Hamlet*, from the first moment is in the magnetic pull of the other world, the grave.

Everything in *Hamlet* tends to this grave. The image of the Ghost on the battlements rising out of it, hurrying to get back at cock's crow, begins the play. At the end, Hamlet, his uncle, mother, Laertes, and the Danish throne, sink into it. The protagonists of *Lear*, the Earl of Gloucester and King Lear, die of exhaustion. The single body of Lear and his daughter dominates the stage a moment; the rest are decorously left to die in the wings. Not so in *Hamlet* where Polonius and then Ophelia's body precede the general pile at the end, draping the boards with blood and cadavers. "'Tis bitter cold, / and I am sick at heart" (FF.1.1:12–13), a guard, unable to see the ghost, yet feeling something of the eerieness on the battlements, volunteers unasked to his relief, only eight lines on in the play. It is a shiver the audience understands as the scenes grind on. In the Second Quarto, Horatio, the rationalist, unbeliever, evokes a world more horrible than the Ghost, out of the chronicles not of his "Philosophy," but of his "History." He sees in Denmark as in ancient Rome, a world haunted by the dead, of zombies hurrying into the street.

> In the most high and palmy state of Rome,
> A little ere the mightiest Julius fell,
> The graves stood tenantless, and the sheeted dead
> Did squeak and gibber in the Roman streets,
> As stars with trains of fire, and dews of blood
> Disasters in the sun; and the moist star,

Upon whose influence *Neptunes* Empire stands,
Was sick almost to doomsday with eclipse.
And even the like precurse of feare[d] events
As harbingers preceding still the fates
And prologue to the *Omen* coming on
Have heaven and earth together demonstrated
Unto our Climatures and countrymen.

(Q2.B2ᵛ:1.1. 113–25)

That phrase "sick almost to doomsday with eclipse" recalls the guard's opening, "I am sick at heart." The echo it sets up is a "harbinger" of the world of evil, dark, cold, the night of the graves opening up in the earth, and sky, exploding, signalling judgment, the final "doomsday."

While Shakespeare cut this speech from the Folio as too rhetorical, external to the ghostly obsession of the Prince, the lines remains for the reader seeking to understand the play in its metamorphosis through the mind of the playwright. The speech is part of Shakespeare's scaffolding for the backdrop he erected on stage in the course of shaping the action. The sentences indicate, as do several others cut from Horatio's speech, the overhanging aura of dread Shakespeare wished to create.[5]

Horatio's words speak not to the return of the dead for revenge. They express the threat of the dark, of the dead, to overwhelm life. Horatio, whose Roman name links him not only to a legend of loyalty, but also to classical augury, twinned to Hamlet like Ophelia with "Prophetic soul," understands it as such. In the case of Caesar, the state was troubled, but here the augury is more personal. Denmark to be sure will totter, but Hamlet the Dane, not the state, is the subject of the drama. Horatio, meeting the dead father a few lines on, intuits that the Ghost may come not to forewarn his country but out of some crime, extortion, "in the womb of Earth." Because Claudius is guilty of his brother's murder, we regard the Ghost as "honest," and so Hamlet characterizes him in his first fit of enthusiasm for the revenge the spirit has set him to. Hamlet has second thoughts however, and so should we.

Horatio, it seems, never quite abandons his first suspicion of the Ghost's malignancy. Throughout the play, Hamlet's remarks to the one friend of his bosom address Horatio's grim doubt. Just before the "mousetrap," Hamlet speaks in terms, which, like his jumping away from the father "moling" under the ground, are clearly irreverent, indicating the Prince's own ambivalence,

It is a damned Ghost that we have seen:
And my Imaginations are as foul
As Vulcans Stythe

(F.F.3.2: 1933–35)

(One might view the whole of the graveyard scene as an attempt by Hamlet to answer Horatio's skepticism as to the Ghost's motives, or at least to dismiss the Ghost as irrelevant to the business at hand— the necessity to kill Claudius before he kills Hamlet.)

The second long cut to the Quarto (pointed out above in the note 5):

The very place puts toys of desperation
Without more motive, into every brain
That looks so many fathoms to the sea
And hears it roar beneath

was excised from the Folio, not only because Shakespeare became convinced that the sense of terror on the battlements was sufficient without it. By offering the place as a reason for Hamlet's being "draw[n . . .] into madness," the audience is distracted from Horatio's intuition that the Ghost, in "depriving" the Prince's "Sovereignty of Reason," is tempting him toward suicide. "Reason" is already suspect in *Hamlet* for we have heard Claudius twist it, but it is still Horatio's measure of truth. "Oh good *Horatio*, I'll take the Ghosts word for a thousand pound," Hamlet cries out as Claudius rushes from the play the prince has staged. The remark betrays Hamlet's anxiety before his friend in the very teeth of the proof. At the play's end, Hamlet speaks about the oppression of the "Augury," about his heart. Is it the warning of the Ghost? Something is speaking to Hamlet from the other world, but it is internalized, "all . . . about" his "heart" (*F.F.* 5.2: 3661–62).[6] Horatio urges Hamlet to listen to his intuition, but this may be Shakespeare's irony, just as he chooses Horatio the skeptic to bring Hamlet news of his father's ghost. How strongly does Horatio urge Hamlet to abandon the fencing match? Horatio remains, until the very end, passive, half paralyzed. He is, however, ready enough to lay hands on the young prince, his friend, at the beginning, and ready to leap after him into suicide at the end. It may indeed be that "all" is about Horatio's heart throughout the play, and that *all* is suspicion of Hamlet's father.

In thinking of *Hamlet*, consider first the plot, what happens, not only what characters say. The fact that staggers is that the Ghost, putatively Hamlet's father, delivers his son to death. This calls into question conventional notions of the play's meaning. If one wonders about Shakespeare's absence—sets aside the stage costumes and scenery, the "majesty of buried Denmark"—and thinks instead about a son and his father, many remarks as well as the action, the revenge, begin to jar.

Is the Ghost malignant? Hamlet, at first sight of his father, exclaims, "Angels and Ministers of Grace defend us." Even as he balances opposites, wondering whether it is "a Spirit of health" or a "Goblin damn'd," the Prince sums with "thou com'st in such a questionable shape."[7] Hamlet has been frightened, his "disposition" shaken "horridly," and this keys his expectation. His speaks of bursting, pulling apart. He consents to call the shape, "*Hamlet*"[8] (in the Folio, the Ghost returns this eerie intimacy, calling his son, "*Hamlet*"), but even as the Prince tries out epithets and intimate address, "King, Father, Royal Dane,"[9] none of which move the Ghost, his verbs marshal his terror, "Let me not burst in Ignorance . . . . thy Canonized bones Hearsed in death, / Have burst their cerments." (This last "Canonized" echoes Hamlet's death wish, "Oh . . . that the Everlasting had not fixt / his *Canon* 'gainst Self-slaughter." The bones in bursting overstep canon.) The ghost makes "Night hideous" and Hamlet and his friends "fools of Nature." This is a threat of the world Horatio describes in the Quarto, Rome before the Day of Judgment, overrun by ghouls.

When the Ghost speaks, it is to confess that he is both father and "Goblin damn'd." He is burning in Hell for "foul crimes," condemned "to fast in Fires." While he claims that it is not immeasurable wickedness, that he is condemned only "Till the foul crimes done in my days of Nature / are burnt and purg'd away?" (*FF*.1.5: 697–98), these crimes are never clear. What one sees is that he exacts from a son the promise of revenge. Yet the Ghost's incarceration up to this point has been terrible. He hints of the horror of "his Prison-House."

. . . . But that I am forbid
To tell the secrets of my Prison-House;
I could a Tale unfold, whose lightest word
Would harrow up thy soul, freeze thy young blood,
Make thy two eyes like Stars, start from their Spheres,
Thy knotty and combined locks to part,
And each particular hair to stand an end
Like Quills upon the fretful Porpentine:

(*FF*.1.5: 698–705)

Why does Hamlet's father threaten to terrify? What does he most resent—his murder or his brother's enjoyment of Gertrude? She, the Ghost seems to wish, to keep in life, but the revenge will entail her death too. A ghost is suspect when it effects additional murders and a dubious justice. Is Hamlet complicit in this? As if he were engendered by a ghost, the father's son sits in the grave.

"Something is rotten in the state of Denmark" (FF.1.4: 678) does not exclude the Prince. Just before the Ghost appears, Hamlet in the Second Quarto speaks, thinking of Claudius, of "some vicious mole of nature" in men, "As in their birth wherein they are not guilty, / (Since nature cannot chose his origin) . . . " (Q2.D: 1.4.24–26), corrupting and poisoning both character and reputation. As the nephew of Claudius, the son of Gertrude, Hamlet must fear the mole within himself, even more after the Ghost's revelations. Hamlet's self-disgust is dangerous to him, an antagonist. Who is the author of this self-disgust, the preoccupation of the play, and, so, finally, Shakespeare's self-disgust? The answer lies less with the mother than the father. In the scene just preceding it, Laertes has warned his sister of the "canker" that "galls the infant of the spring" and "contagious blastments." Ophelia's father will shortly *do* that. It is no accident then that Hamlet calls his father, the Ghost, in a moment of mockery "old Mole" shortly after he has characterized the evil corrupting the outwardly fair aspect of the anonymous man who sounds like Claudius as a mole. In the scene directly after the Ghost appears to Hamlet, Polonius works like a mole to discover his son's character, blemishing and cankering Laertes' reputation in the process. That the mole is literally a creature of the underworld, of the grave, links them all—Polonius, Claudius, the Ghost—in Hamlet's mind. The mole is a form of worm in this respect, a mammalian worm. This fear of being corrupted, is instilled by the fathers in *Hamlet*. But *they* are the personification of it. The only answer then is to go down and wrestle with the father in the grave.

Prince Hamlet's first unconstrained breath, the court having left him alone on the stage, rushes toward the rank world of weeds, ditches, rot, mucous, the underworld wishing to disappear into the earth.

> O that this too too sullied[10] flesh would melt,
> Thaw and resolve itself into a dew,
> Or that the everlasting had not fixt
> His canon gainst seal slaughter, o God, God,
> How wary, stale, flat, and unprofitable

Seem to me all the uses of this world:
Fie on't, ah fie, tis an unweeded garden
That grows to seed, things rank and gross in nature,
Possess it merely that it should come thus

(Q2.C: 1.2.129–137)

Does only "canon," church law, keep Hamlet from suicide? This *is* excessive grief, and Claudius's smug homilies, "your Father lost a Father, / That Father lost, lost his . . . ", ring almost sensible. Can Hamlet's mother in her dexterous speed to "Incestuous sheets" have sickened him so? The anger that Hamlet first deflects on himself, then on his mother, has a deeper source. The displacement of anger at another on to oneself is identified by Freud as the source of suicide. In the Prince's stream of rage there is the desire to be *absent*, not to be part either of the world or the family. Hamlet's curse on seed and his own breeding in his first soliloquy sounds a theme he will develop, the commonality of all flesh decomposed in the grave. Hamlet's anger is deliberately overstated. (Would he in public chide Gertrude at the drama's inception as lower than a "beast that wants discourse of Reason"?) Hamlet ought not to be considering suicide then, but rebuking his mother. Why is it that the inheritance has not fallen to the son who is clearly of age? How deeply Hamlet resents this is not fully revealed until the very end of the play: "Popt in between th' election and my hopes" (F.F.5.2: 3569).[11] Why has the old king not prepared his son's succession better? Why, in the breath before, does Hamlet refer not to his father but to "my King?" ("Does it not, thinkst thee, stand me now upon / He that hath kill'd my King, and whor'd my Mother, / Popt in between th' election and my hopes. . . .")

Ernst Jones has discussed Hamlet's strong Oedipal motives, the desire to murder the King his father and to sleep with his mother, Gertrude. If this is his secret, Hamlet will identify with Claudius and find himself incapable of action against the latter. These remarks are hardly half the story. One of this literary psychiatrist's observations is characteristic not only of his thesis but also of his perspective: "The play is mainly concerned with a hero's unavailing fight against what can only be called a disordered mind."[12] No wonder psychiatry can neither see nor understand the Ghost, any more than Gertrude could. The Ghost is certainly real. Horatio, the soldiers on the battlements as well as Hamlet see it. Why the disparity? (The early watch, who has not seen it, reports its brooding presence in physiological terms: "I am sick at heart.") The answer is simple. Gertrude is insensitive to evil. Her marriage proves it. She has to be forced to look into her heart, soul, for "black and grained spots."

The Ghost is real; it is not a "disordered mind" that Hamlet wages war against, but a "disordered universe." The reduction of Hamlet to childhood fantasies of sexual intimacy with his mother reduces the play to a barbarous infancy (as it indeed reduces the Greek drama *Oedipus*). Yet the notion of Hamlet's mind as the stage of the tragedy is perspicacious. Hamlet and his shadow, Horatio, are thinkers, reasoners, men in whom philosophy, reflection, is not only a good, but perhaps the highest. "O what a Noble mind is here o're-throwne?" Ophelia exclaims (*FF*.3.2: 1806). Coleridge comments on the interior world of thought that marks the hero: "This admirable and consistent character, deeply acquainted with his own feelings, painting them with such wonderful power and accuracy, and firmly persuaded that a moment ought not to be lost in executing the solemn charge committed to him, still yields to the same retiring from reality, which is the result of having, what we express by the terms, a world within himself."[13] Yes, "A world within himself" for the play may be seen as a macrocosm of Hamlet's head, thoughts, dreams, psychology, even, since we are speaking of ghosts—soul.

Hatred and love, are crossed with understanding in the mind of the Prince. He embraces with mockery, as he departs for England, the usurping uncle as father/mother. Hamlet projects Shakespeare's awareness of the complexities of father and son onto the largest possible stage. Like Lear in the storm scene, Hamlet sees his agony reflected from the skies, shaking the earth, planets. If for a moment the Prince is caught in the toils of Freud, desiring to murder his father and sleep with mother, he is an auditor of his own state of mind. Perhaps amusement with such a thought sheds light on that strangest of lines, which is assumed to be sarcasm but which may be instead self-recognition. Claudius, in act 4, scene 3, informing Hamlet that he must depart, hears in response to his command that the Prince quit Denmark posthaste for England the latter's cheerful, "Good." Claudius can not resist the cynical flash of "So it is, if thou knew'st our purposes." He knows what we do not: that sealed letters condemn his nephew to death on landing. But Hamlet turns this upside down with his trump, "I see a Cherub that see's him: but come, for / England. Farewell, dear Mother."

Claudius is rightly confused, both by the warning that a cherub sits on Hamlet's shoulder and sees into Claudius's mind and by being addressed as "dear Mother," as if he is Gertrude.

"Thy loving Father *Hamlet*," the King cloyingly corrects.

"My Mother: Father and Mother is man and / wife: man & wife is one flesh, and so my mother. Come, / for England" (*FF.*4.3: 2710–17).

The sardonic insult, "Mother," which Hamlet twice offers, warns Claudius of unriddling the Prince's state of mind in pat formula. On the basest level, he is calling the King a woman, a coward, not a man. In another sense he is ignoring Claudius as a man, a king, and bidding him good-bye only as an adjunct of his mother. At the very same moment, he is parodying the tenderness with which Claudius must honey his "if thou knew'st our purposes," by saying good-bye to him with the emotion one might show to a mother as opposed to a father. Far more provocative, however, is Hamlet's refusal to call Claudius, "Dear Father" by calling him "dear Mother." Yet in context, the jest has a grimmer riddle to propound. It is an apt statement of Hamlet's dilemma, proof that he is aware of where he is and must go. That is why, in the bleakness, "for England" is a hopeful cry. Finally, he calls no one "Dear Father"—nor can he. "Perturbed spirit" and "gracious figure" are the kindest encomiums he has for the Ghost.

Just before he has been brought in to Claudius who has demanded of him, "Where's Polonius?"

"At Supper," the Prince snaps or jests.

"At Supper? Where?"

Is it possible that Polonius is alive? After all, no one but Gertrude and Hamlet have seen the corpse.

"Not where he eats, but where he is eaten, a cer- / tain convocation of worms are e'ne at him. Your worm / is your only Emperor for diet. We fat all creatures else / to fat us, and we fat ourself for Maggots. Your fat King, / and your lean Beggar is but variable service t[w]o dishes, / but to one Table that's the end" (*FF.* 4.3: 2685–90).

In the Second Quarto, Claudius cries, "Alas, alas." From his exclamation one may suppose for a moment, again, that Claudius is fooled into wondering if Hamlet is mad with this word salad in his mouth. But Hamlet's next line disabuses him. "A man may fish with the worm that hath eat of a King, & / eat of the fish that hath fed of that worm" (*Q2.K2:* 4.3.26–28). The exchange was cut from the Folio, where "fat King" and "lean Beggar," evidently served well enough to signal Hamlet's meaning.[14]

To either of these lines, the Folio or Second Quarto's, their veiled threat, Claudius is attentive. "What dost thou mean by this?"

"Nothing but to show you how a King may go / a Progress through the guts of a Beggar." The acid sting of this line is double.

It mocks Claudius's pretensions to "divinity," the aura that surrounds and sanctifies royalty. (This is the very height of Claudius's hypocrisy, the regicide who can nervously pronounce, "There's such Divinity doth hedge a King, / That Treason can but peep to what it would, / Acts little of his will" [FF.4.5: 2868–70].) The riddle of the king who goes through the belly of a beggar also warns Claudius that Hamlet knows all, not from Heaven, but from the world of the grave. In particular the Prince knows the worm, again in its double sense of sexual desire and conscience that works in the guts of his uncle.

"Two dishes . . . to one table," echoes the remark about "variable service" that Hamlet made to Horatio at the very beginning of the play: "the Funeral-Bakt meats / Did coldly furnish forth the Marriage Tables" (FF.1.2.368–69). It is the humor of the grave. "A certain convocation of politic worms" (Q2.K2: 4.3.20) sneers at Polonius's colleagues of the Danish court. Ostensibly Hamlet's riddles emphasize the mutability and vulnerability of all flesh. The accusation—you have eaten my father and this kingdom, "we fat ourself for maggots"—is not heard by the King until Hamlet, literally, in the Quarto, hooks the worm. The conundrum of a worm eating of a king, being eaten by yet another creature that is being "angled" for in turn draws the King's attention. He no longer cries over his nephew's madness, but inquires directly the meaning. When Hamlet draws it—that a king may be eaten—go through the guts of a beggar—Claudius reverts to, "Where is *Polonius*?" Hamlet's answer, under the pretence of a riddle, enables him to insult with brutal directness. He tells the King to send to Heaven to find Polonius: "If your Messen- / ger find him not there, seek him i'th other place your / self." It is a transparent euphemism for "go to Hell." To this is added the further ignominy of Hamlet's image of the King running up against the corpse of Polonius with his nose: "you / shall nose him as you go up the stairs into the Lobby" (FF.4.5: 2697–98). It implies that the King has a nose for stench, like a rat, but, worse, that Claudius, crawling, on his belly like a worm, a maggot, will push up against the prostrate Polonius.

It is not into dew, then, that "this too too solid Flesh" will resolve itself, but into food for maggots—not etherealization but the table fare of maggots, rottenness. Hamlet too has become a maggot, eating Polonius—the identity of all flesh is one of the constituents of his joke. The "Farewell dear Mother" while hinting that Claudius is only his father through his sexual union with his mother—no father, in truth, and no king—further riddles that as uncle and nephew, Hamlet and Claudius are practically one flesh too; all

flesh is kin—and the mystery of the sexual union in which two
become one makes one out of two of them (with the union of all
flesh in maggotry). It recalls another tenderness that Hamlet offers
his uncle in the middle of the play: "Your Majesty, and we that
have free souls, it touches / us not." There is some fellowship in
that, under the obvious irony, Claudius wishes to be free and so
does Hamlet—free from very different and yet similar burdens.
(Recognize, as Hamlet does, that Claudius has a strong conscience.
Without it, the device of the play would never work, for it would
not "touch" him.) They are "mighty opposites" (*FF*.5.2: 3565) as
Hamlet points out in disparaging the underlings who do the King's
bidding. They are sharers in Gertrude's flesh. If the trauma of
Hamlet, as the critic, Bradley, sees it, is his mother's responsibility
for the tragedy—her corruption (at least as it appears so to her son)
in Claudius's arms—it is not their common lust, but their common
decay that Hamlet's language evokes. Flesh is food for maggots,
corruptible, infected with sin, as Claudius remarks, taking in his
own odor, "rank, it smells to heaven" (*FF*.3.3: 2312).

This is the Ghost's perspective. Hamlet's vision is disordered
only if the ghost is not real. But Denmark in the play *Hamlet* is
rotten, the contagion of the grave everywhere. If Hamlet lived elsewhere, it might be a play of conscience. But Hamlet is subject to the
ghost, seen by his friends as real, and the vision Horatio speaks of
in the Second Quarto, a world in which the dead wander at will,
drawing the living to their purposes.

The "sullied flesh" of the Quarto gives way in the Folio to hallucinated flesh. At this point in the play nothing seems real or
"solid" to Hamlet. His joking about the commonality of flesh has
taken the Prince into the grave. No wonder that the older Shakespeare cut most of the lines in which Hamlet muses on Fortinbras's
will to action (see pp. 64–65). The tenor of the speech is out of keep-
ing with Hamlet's grisly perspective. At this moment the Prince
has already answered the questions posed in his dialogue with
Claudius. Flesh is no longer solid. The grip of his father is complete.

The drama within the drama is the Prince's struggle to be free
of his father. The shifting back and forth on the stage, as if to escape even while swearing his friends on oath in their first crucial
meeting, is Shakespeare's first pointer.

The action is comic, and the language in which he addresses the
Ghost, acknowledged now as his father, "old Mole,"[15] is meant to
underscore this. The conventional response, however, is to hear
the breathless call to revenge of Hamlet. "Escape?" one of my audi-
tors questions. "Not pursuit? 'I'll make a Ghost of him that lets

me' " (*FF*.1.4: 672). But this is uttered precisely at the moment *before* Hamlet knows anything, *before* he is told the tale of his father's murder and sworn by the ghost to revenge. Once he hears the tale, his behavior is hardly that of a man in pursuit. Whatever he says, the stage action belies it, deliberately contradicting the image of a man in hot pursuit, almost making Hamlet's vow ludicrous.

Hamlet swears his friends on the battlement not to what he ought to, revenge, but to silence. When the Ghost lends his voice to Hamlet's, the Prince begins to mock him:

> *Gho.* Swear (*Ghost cries under the Stage*).
> *Ham.* Ah ha boy, say'st thou so. Art thou there true-
> penny? Come one [on] you hear this fellow in the cellarage
> Consent to swear.
>
> (*FF*.1.5: 845–48)

What Hamlet has done in fact is to call the "honest Ghost's" reality into question, stripping away the stage machinery, exposing it as an actor under the stage. This is no flippant confidence to the audience in a quick aside but an act of reckless boldness on Shakespeare's part as if he wanted to rend the fabric of belief, interrupt the tension, ridicule it. There are parallels, the drunken porter, for instance, in *Macbeth*, but there the buffoonery does not destroy the concentration of the murderer, the central actor in the drama.

Comic interruption is a way of heightening the suspense of the murder, manipulating the tension in the audience. Here Hamlet, himself, seems to find the stage tension too great. This is radical, "modern," a self-aware question about life and theater. It recalls Pirandello's *Six Characters in Search of an Author* and Cervantes's positioning of Don Quixote between fictional adventure and the reality of the novel. The burlesque in *Hamlet*, however, is neither "literary" as in Cervantes's second volume of *Quixote*, nor the overt theme of the drama as in Pirandello. Hamlet's is compelled by the drama. What is Shakespeare's reason for putting the whole revenge tragedy into jeopardy, doubt, just as it begins with an almost crude lampoon on his own stage technique? Something about that cry from the "cellarage" jostles Shakespeare and the Prince into an antic madness. Hamlet begins to run, shift his ground, visibly trying to escape the ghost:

> *Hor.* Propose the Oath my Lord.
> *Ham.* Never to speak of this that you have seen,

Swear by my sword.
Gho. Swear.
Ham. Hic et ubique? Then we'll shift for ground,
Come hither Gentlemen,
And lay your hands again upon my sword,
Never to speak of this that you have heard:
Swear by my Sword.
Gho. Swear.
Ham. Well said old Mole, can'st work i'th' ground so fast?
A worthy Pioneer, once more remove good friends.

(FF.1.5: 849–60)

Three times Hamlet removes, shifts away from the spot from where the Ghost cries. (One can assume that the *hic et ubique* has followed a shift of Hamlet's and not the Ghost's.) It is not until the fourth "swear" of the Ghost that Hamlet returns to a conventional response, calling out what one might have expected to hear the first time: "Rest, rest perturbed Spirit" (FF.1.5: 879).

Hamlet wants to act with a whole conscience, but, quite irrespective of his feelings toward his mother, guilt, lust, he cannot—and for reasons that have nothing to do with conflicting impulses. The events of the play prevent him until the very end. He is a creature of bad, even (since the Ghost exists), malignant luck. His grimmest soliloquy speaks exactly to this point: "To be, or not to be. . . ." The same anger and dread drives Hamlet toward two acts, murder and self-murder, revenge and suicide. The conscience that restrains him from resolving his "too, too solid" Flesh into a Dew, breaking the Canon against Self-slaughter, is the Conscience that restrains him from murdering Claudius. The Polonius family acts out in the subplot Hamlet's two murderous impulses, which are really one, unrestrained by conscience: Ophelia and Laertes—the former undertakes suicide, the latter revenge through any means. Lack of conscience characterizes them both at their worst,[16] while conscience is the distinguishing mark of Hamlet. To cavil against him as a man who can not make up his mind is to miss the point. He, as against every other major character—Gertrude, Claudius, Polonius, Ophelia, Laertes—is a creature of conscience. Hamlet calls Gertrude back to her conscience and discovers that Ophelia has a weak one. "Get thee to a Nunnery" is not sarcastic but sound advice. Even Claudius struggles with his conscience; in fact, it saves his life. But Claudius can't stick it. He returns to plotting, and this destroys him. The bombast of Laertes's pledge of vengeance is *comic*, a parody of Hamlet's, and therefore a warning of what Hamlet would sound like without conscience: "To hell Allegiance: Vows to the blackest devil / Conscience and Grace, to the profundest Pit. / I dare Damnation" (*FF*.4.5: 2878–80).

The riddle that a man must sometimes die for his conscience is not hard to understand, only painful. Seeing it acted out slowly, it is difficult to bear—that, for what I conceive as finest in me, I may pay with the price of my life.

*   *   *

Why write out of such a sense of pain? Shakespeare's absence is willful in *Hamlet* and *Lear*. Setting aside the royal trappings in the drama, what appears is the son's fear of his father, a father begging from the grave. The Ghost urges the Prince to the deed of murder, but Hamlet constructs instead a trap for the Ghost as much as for Claudius. The Prince alternates between anger and suspicion. This is the burden of one his longest, most poignant soliloquies, "O what a Rogue and Peasant slave am I" (*FF*.2.2: 1590). Why? Again and again Hamlet reiterates, he does not trust the shade that calls itself his father. If Horatio is so scathing to the latter that he offends the specter, Hamlet is even more so. "The Spirit that I have seen / May be the Devil" (*FF*.2.2: 1638). Claudius's guilt draws one away from the obvious conclusion. Hamlet falls into his own mousetrap. ("Not a Mouse stirring," the guard's response in the opening lines of the play, has overtones in this regard.) Hamlet catches Claudius but not the Ghost. The Prince has only half of the truth: he forgets his own question in the contrivance of the trap.

> . . . the Devil hath power
> T'assume a pleasing shape, yea and perhaps
> Out of my Weakness, and my Melancholy,
> As he is very potent with such Spirits,
> Abuses me to damn me. . . .
>
> (*FF*.2.2: 1639–43)

Moving quickly to his revenge after the mousetrap springs, Hamlet finds Claudius on his knees in prayer. Since to strike a conscious blow in such circumstances would make a mockery of the Prince's agonies of conscience before, he withdraws his knife. He waits for the second chance, which seems to come with the rustling in the arras in Gertrude's bedroom. But the stabbing of Polonius turns Hamlet into a murderer. It loses him first his bride, then his life. Where is his protector, the Ghost?

If Hamlet had stabbed Claudius, kneeling in the midst of prayers, would he be no better than the latter? (The fact that Claudius rises, unshriven, is only a cruel twist.) If the answer cannot be yes, one is meant to ask the question, and Shakespeare reminds the audience of it when he has Claudius say to Laertes, "No place indeed should murder Sanctuarize; / Revenge should have no bounds" (FF.4.7: 3117–18). This is the language of a usurper not a king. More important than Hamlet's missed opportunity to revenge is his failure to look behind the arras before he stabs, the folly of stabbing into it, blindly. His exclamation "a Rat?" is surely a joke on Shakespeare's part, for Hamlet's delicate "mousetrap" has not been set for such game. (It is only a mousetrap not a rat-trap, meant to spring on a conscience not to hold a malefactor for justice.) The angry cry at Gertrude's continued betrayal of his confidence, her willingness to shelter spies, stabs himself and his cause. It is a cowardly way to kill Claudius and not a conscious one. The refusal to draw the curtain on his opponent is significant. He does not wish to look upon him, accuse him. There is fear in this, and one may wonder is it Claudius[17] whom Hamlet is stabbing, or the fluttering shape in the curtains, which could as well be, and may suggest, the Ghost.

Hamlet has been caught in a situation, a "mousetrap," that must spring on him. The Ghost's appearance after the killing of Polonius is peculiar. Here the son has just stabbed Polonius, thinking, at least consciously, that it is Claudius, and the father chides him for "blunted purpose," the blood still on the Prince's knife. Most of the Ghost's lines have to do with Gertrude. One must consider again the hesitation of Hamlet. The Ghost's, the shadow father's, prescription has been impossible to fulfill: "Taint not thy mind; nor let thy Soul contrive / Against thy Mother ought; leave her to heaven . . ." (FF.1.5: 770–71). But the son's mind *is* tainted, how can it help but be? Does his mother prove her innocence, wittingly or unwittingly, by swallowing poison? (On the question of Gertrude's knowledge the First Quarto, Second Quarto, and Folio differ widely.) Finally it is not Gertrude but Laertes who gives the crucial testimony against the King. Hamlet never does forgive Gertrude. She may be guiltless of the plot against his father, but not of lechery. His hardly tender good-bye is "wretched Queen, adieu"; there is still a flash of his sexual resentment in the way he administers the final draught to Claudius, forcing the poison down his throat, in a parody of communion, the adjective, "incestuous" smacking against "Union."

Here thou incestuous, murd'rous,
Damned Dane,

Drink off this Potion: Is thy Union here?
Follow my Mother.

                                        (*FF*.5.2: 3807–10)

Given the riddle, does Hamlet solve it? Stand back from the character and look at the play, Shakespeare's play. While Hamlet can not avoid death, he does manage to free himself from the Ghost. *This* is the riddle that Shakespeare was interested in. The death of his hero, the Prince, was a foregone conclusion. The play solves the riddle by descending into the very medium of the Ghost. Shakespeare can not, as Dante can, in the pages of poetry, take his hero through the underworld. He does, however, after Hamlet's return from the high seas, send him down into the grave.

The long scene with the clowns in the graveyard, shovelling, scooping, throwing up skulls, bones, is the center of gravity in *Hamlet*. It is in this hole that the answer comes to the question the Hamlet of the Second Quarto raised as he left for England, Fortinbras's valor:

The imminent death of twenty thousand men,
That for a fantasy and trick of fame
Go to their graves like beds, fight for a plot
Whereon the numbers cannot try the cause,
Which is not tomb enough and continent
To hide the slain

                                        (*Q2*.K3^v: 4.4.60–65)

Hamlet's response to the question of honor, greatness, at that moment, can only be considered ironic: "Rightly to be great, / Is not to stir without great argument, / But greatly to find quarrel in a straw / When honor's at the stake" (*Q2*.K3^v: 4.4.53–56). But honor is a "fantasy and trick of fame." The waste of life for it remains appalling, despite the Prince's apostrophe to "bloody" thoughts.

It is telling that, in the Folio, Hamlet's lines to Horatio about Fortinbras are cut from this scene, reducing it from sixty-six lines to nine. Why did Shakespeare choose to cut four, four so drastically? Hamlet's lines here do not represent what he has thought or will think, and the need to be ironic, to answer directly the questions of action, honor, etc., was no longer important to Shakespeare. Fortinbras as hero, even without the Folio's cuts, is hardly credible. The Norwegian prince is only a shadow in the play, and his actions are not a possible alternative to Hamlet's. Prince Hamlet's speech in the Quarto seems to take the Norwegian prince and his will to act seriously, even though Shakespeare's tongue was obviously in his cheek throughout the description of Fortinbras and the military campaign against Poland for "a little patch of ground / that hath in it no profit. . . ." "To find quarrel in a straw / when honor's at the stake": the remarks were too close to Polonius's remarks about a quarrel (despite the substitution of rashness for prudence as the motivating principle). "Exposing. . .for an Egg-shell. . . . a fantasy and trick of fame": Hamlet's words belie the admiration they express, but they *seem* to be self-criticism by the Danish prince. Shakespeare may have seen that in the audience's reactions and felt again the danger of his epigrams being taken at face value. The long speech is better cut, not only to avoid misinterpretation, but also for the sake of the swift development of the action.

The Hamlet who returns from the sea voyage is "naked" as he writes to Claudius of all illusions, not only of honor but of life. It is the answer of the dead, a man resigned, whose perspective is from the grave towards life. Death is not horrid, as the Ghost suggests but "felicity," as Hamlet jokes dying, to Horatio, asking the latter to "absent" himself from that happiness, "felicity awhile" (*FF.* 5.2: 3833).[18] It is fitting that Hamlet has previously descended into an actual grave and joked with the clowns digging it.

The clowns who poke in the earth, jesting, drinking, possibly stumbling—their like will not be seen on the stage until the twentieth century and Beckett. It is with a certain shock of self-recognition that Hamlet watches their deliberate merrymaking over death: "Ha's this fellow no feeling of his business, that / he sings at Grave-making?" (*FF.*5.1: 3256–57).

This is a description, however, of Hamlet himself. Horatio's answer, "Custom hath made it in him a property of ea- / siness," is an evasion. The clowns play with the bones make Hamlet's own "ache to think / on't . . ." (*FF.*5.1: 3282–83) for the graveyard vaudevillians are juggling a buffoon subtext to his own fooling. Skull after skull comes flying from the grave. A kind of fury attends the shoveling of the gravediggers as they knock the cadavers about, the same anger Hamlet has felt against the dead. So Yorick, the old king's fool, is made to snap the jaws of his skull, resurrected. The joking goes on. It seems simple-minded. Its function is not so much to entertain as to draw attention to Hamlet's position, in the grave, his own grave, without being dead. Out of life, yet not in death. The ambition with which he began the play must be resigned. Fortinbras's example "honor" in a "straw" is mocked succinctly:

Ham. Dost thou think *Alexander* looked o' this fa-
shion i'th' earth?
Hor. E'ene so.
Ham. And smelt so? Puh.

(FF.5.1: 3385–88)

Alexander's "Noble dust" will ultimately, if you trace its disper-
sions into the elements, time, history, be found "stopping a bung-
hole." It is to such uses rather than dew that flesh "resolves itself."
Hamlet declaims in a parody of poetry, his own comic death song:

> Imperial *Caesar*, dead and turned to clay,
> Might stop a hole to keep the wind away.

In this gibing at the backside, there is contempt not only for life
but also for death, the world of bones and ghost. The play has
passed some boundary, and there will be no more ghostly inter-
ventions.

Henceforth, Hamlet will watch events unfold with such grim
resignation that one imagines that he has become the old Hamlet,
the King, a ghost rather than a man of flesh and blood. A moment
later he will learn that Ophelia has gone to the land of the dead.
"A Ministering Angel," Laertes proclaims, and indeed her death
ministers to Hamlet for it is into her grave that he leaps to proclaim
himself king: "This is I, / *Hamlet* the Dane" (*FF.*5.1: 3452–53).

The cry must make a shiver go up the back of Claudius. But now,
Hamlet surprises all. He challenges Laertes to indeed be buried
alive.

> . . . Dost thou come here to whine;
> To outface me with leaping in her Grave?
> Be buried quick with her, and so will I.
> And if thou prate of Mountains; let them throw
> Millions of Acres[19] on us, till our ground
> Singeing his pate against the burning Zone,
> Make *Ossa* like a wart. Nay, and thoul't mouth,
> I'll rant as well as thou.

(FF.5.1: 3474–81)

They will be buried alive together: Laertes like Hamlet overwhelmed by a father's revenge, though no ghost compels him to
it. Hamlet has asked why men go to their graves like "beds" over
"straws." Now he stands in Ophelia's grave, his bed, understanding he will be tumbled into it. He resents Laertes for speaking as

if he understood the grave. The exaggeration of the latter's language, its pretentiousness, betrays an adolescent. This is true not only in the graveyard, where Hamlet scolds like a sarcastic schoolmaster, but also at the conclusion of the fencing match. Poisoned in treachery, Hamlet blinks at Laertes's last words, asking forgiveness, answering, "Heaven make thee free of it." Heaven, the realm of the unknown, the dead, not man forgives murder. (In mentioning Heaven, though, Hamlet with regal sarcasm indicate good wishes to his murderer.) Hamlet's words are the wisdom of a man whose life is not taking place in the commonplace world of facts.

Is this why Hamlet has no prescience about Laertes's intentions toward him, which ought to be obvious? He can remark to Horatio, ". . . by the image of my Cause, I see / The Portraiture of his" (*FF*.5.2: 3581–82). Hardly—the images are only superficially the same. The murder of Polonius and Hamlet's father are certainly different. The very language of portraiture, of painted reality, warns of a lie. Hamlet sees only his own situation; Laertes's point of view he sees not at all. If he did—what could he do? Kill Laertes? Take him into confidence? Laertes is not aware of the sickness of Denmark any more than his father, Polonius.

It is just one of the insoluble riddles that Hamlet is set. "Why, what a King is this?" Horatio exclaims when the Prince describes how he has dispatched to death his traitorous former friends, Guildenstern and Rosencrantz (*FF*.5.2: 3566). Horatio's outburst of praise is not merely for the deed, but also for the tone of Hamlet's voice, the "Authority" (as Kent puts it to Lear, returning as Caius for service): "'Tis dangerous, when the baser nature comes / Between the pass, and fell incensed points / Of mighty opposites" (*FF*.5.2: 3563–65). It is not only to kill Claudius that Hamlet is bound, but also to succeed to the throne. By fleeing the play, Claudius has cheated him of a chance for public denunciation, and by kneeling for private revenge.

Hamlet acts when he can act, sometimes as with Polonius, simply stabbing. The proper moment is given to him in death, poisoned, where but a few moments are allotted to him to fulfill revenge and claim election. He "seizes the day." But he seizes it as a dead man, a ghost. The revenge is immediately overshadowed by the dying of King Hamlet. (This is staged with a skill in the Olivier film, which serves this argument. Hamlet takes his seat in the throne, moves, as a stiffening ghost in the stately charade of his final, royal moments, at last, the king.) He has the briefest of reigns. We watch on stage the fable of time and the futility of human glory, a dumb show set before us in the Prince's accession and death—two, three minutes, a lifetime. It freezes our blood. As a Prince merely, Hamlet's death could never have moved us as it does, the instant after he has cried out, "Let the door be lock'd," seizing the court, the crown, Denmark. In death, the testimony of his own poisoning and the Queen's (almost on that condition), Hamlet has forced the corrupt court to acquiesce, to finally be jury and judge to Claudius's treachery. Hamlet's disdain is not for power, what Alexander has sought, but for the meaning of power in time. It is the short-lived Alexander he speaks of in the grave-yard, and the betrayed Caesar, both summed in him.

The Ghost visibly absent from the last scene does not return to gloat—wisely. The audience might pelt—or hoot—it, if not a "Goblin damn'd," certainly a nightshade. Hamlet has exorcised it in the graveyard, or rather, Shakespeare has. But it has cost Hamlet his own solid flesh, reality.

No one who is sensitive to absence, Shakespeare's, certainly, can fail to note the curious calm towards the end of the play, following Hamlet's return from England. Despite the "Towering passion" Hamlet speaks of later and his antics in leaping into Ophelia's plot beside her brother, the Prince's reaction to Laertes's ranting, "brav-ery," is that of a man who is not merely controlled, but actually removed in his emotions. No ghost comes to haunt the Prince, to stir him, to remind him. This makes one almost reconsider the very notion of the malignant father. Hamlet, goes down into the grave, but he has recovered his equanimity somewhere else. The Prince is no longer fighting for his father but for himself. He understands that Claudius wishes to kill him. Claudius's trap of the English trip has worked to Hamlet's advantage, and he has proof, not of Claudius's or his mother's complicity in a father's death, but in the single plot of Claudius for Hamlet's own death.

So he awaits his moment; it comes, he strikes! It is his affair now, not his father's. He is his father: "This is I, / *Hamlet* the Dane." (How mocking, to proclaim it standing in a grave, staring up at Claudius.) Somewhere between the threat of the early acts and the calm of the final ones, the interior tragedy, drama, has been resolved. Shakespeare has met his own ghost, his father, and made his peace.[20] The truth of the play *Hamlet* lies out of sight, on the high seas, where freshened by a breeze, by action, the Prince is able to shake off or take within his own character the threatening Ghost. The unlikely physician who predicted, "Haply the Seas . . . shall expel / This something settled matter in his heart: / Whereon his Brains still beating, puts him thus / From fashion of himself" has spoken wisely.[21] Perhaps there is some piquant reflection of this in the gravedigger's observation that either England will cure Hamlet of madness or that he will not seem mad given the temper of the English population: "he shall recover his / wits there; or if he do not, it's no great matter there. . . . / 'Twill not be seen in him, there the men are as / mad as he" (FF.5.1: 3341–42, 3344–45). It is not a cure of madness that the journey towards England effects, but a coming to terms with it, oneself, the irrational, father, mother, uncle, the kingship, the necessity of considered action. Under the superficial jest of the clown/gravedigger that the English are all crazy is a more serious reflection. All men who live in a world of self-reflection live at a level of intensity and doubt that mimics the apprehensions of insanity. The gravedigger began digging on the day of Hamlet's birth. That day was the same on which the old Hamlet, his father, "overcame *Fortinbras.*" The scrape of the shovel toward death, the triumphant moment of the old king, the birth of the son, are made coincidental by the playwright. Hamlet's sea voyage brings him to a grave in which birth and death, songs of love and lament, join. It is no accident that it is the king's jester whose skull Hamlet recovers in the grave and whom he speaks of with a fondness we never hear him express towards his father: "he / hath born me on his back a thousand times" (FF.5.1: 3373–74). If Yorick is not his true father, surely he is one of his teachers. The antic disposition of the Prince seen in his banter in the grave becomes almost merry. Despite the "ill" (Second Quarto) about his heart, he can jest with Osric, ducking and bowing in a parody of the latter. This speaks to the sea voyage that has ended his soliloquies, made him confident of a true friend in Horatio, and put him into a good humor that neither the threats of Laertes or his own death can shake, witness the jest of "felicity." By going to a land of insanity, Hamlet has become sane, without even landing there. Letter in hand, he has a document from his voyage that testifies to Claudius's evil, not the impression of a "psycho-drama." The story for the Prince is no longer a revenge tragedy. It is a battle for his own life.

The riddle of the tragedy remains. Was the specter, the father, responsible for the child's death? The father may retort, I came to warn you, and the son reply, it was your warning that put my life in jeopardy. Had I remained distant, absent, letting the king "of shreds and patches" enjoy his "reechy kisses," I might have come to the throne in my own good time, with my mother's management. Could Hamlet indeed have escaped Claudius's poison given the threat he posed as "the most immediate to our Throne" and the rightful heir in the former's conscience? Is it in fact the disappearance of the Ghost that leaves Hamlet vulnerable to Claudius, the voice of warning reduced to a mere sensation of uneasiness, "how ill all's here about my heart . . . a kind of gamgiving, as / would perhaps trouble a woman" (Q2.N3ᵛ: 5.2.201–2; 204–5)? Is it folly on his part to "defy Augury?" Although the tone is cocky, the mood almost ebullient, is not the remark, "What is't to leave be- / times? [early]" (FF.5.2: 3672–73) just before the fencing match that the heartache warns him about, the same sentiment as the longing for suicide in his first soliloquy?

The idea is the same, but the emotion, the sentiment in which it is uttered, is quite different. *Hamlet*, like *Lear*, comes "full circle." Calm, without rancor or self-hatred, Hamlet is prepared for, almost embraces, death. Having descended into the grave, he does not "Seek for" his "Noble Father in the dust." He awaits him, however; "readiness is all." He is locked in the same self-absorption with his dead father in which he was found in the first scene, which Claudius and Gertrude chided. Now, he has in truth, "Within" what "passes show." When he tries to speak of it to Horatio, he has to employ the language of faith about the Heavenly Father's care, watchfulness, seeing his imminent death as a gift of his father, the king, now become one with the Father of All: ". . .there's a special / Providence in the fall of a sparrow" (FF.5.2: 3668–69) (cf. Matthew 10:29: "Are not two sparrows sold for a farthing? and one of them shall not fall on the ground without your Father.").

The answers lie in Heaven, as the final lines of the play make clear. Here, as in *King Lear*, lies "felicity." Here is the secret of why Gertrude posted with such speed to Claudius's sheets, here the reconciliation of father and son, father and daughter. In *Hamlet*, as in *Lear*, the faithful disciple of the agony, Horatio, (answering to Kent) prepares to follow the martyr. He is stayed a moment, to tell the story, the gospel of a transfixed humanity. These powerful fathers, summoning, following their children to other worlds, balance in this present world—against the hope of a gentle Messiah— an older, sterner, wisdom. It is not Lear, Hamlet's father, that Shakespeare finally meditates on in such drama, but fatherhood, his own, his father's. In doing so, at the outer limits, it is with the Father of the Universe, Mysterious Personality after which the religious imagination grasps, that he finds himself.

5

The Shadow's Dance

THE shadow dance with the Ghost, the most important thread of *Hamlet*, was not so apparent to the playwright of the Quarto of 1605, the so-called, Second Quarto,[1] or of the First Quarto of 1603.

The Ghost, the ghostly: these keys unlock the first striking revision at the beginning of the Folio. The flesh in the Quarto was "too too sallied" (*Q2.C*; usually emended, as in the Pelican Shakespeare version, 1.2.129, to "sullied"). In the Folio, Hamlet's flesh is "too too solid" (*FF.*1.2: 313). Shakespeare, revising, wished to dissolve not Hamlet's disgust but his reality in the stage action. The Folio chooses the exact opposite of liquid or tears, that is "solid." The Quarto's adjective "sullied" has to do with washing and purity. It does not convey as "solid" does the sense of flesh anchored to reality.

Horatio uses a careful, slightly skeptical phrase for the reality of the Ghost, "present Object." In a few stage moments, Hamlet will meet the "Object" of his wish, the Ghost, who is indeed flesh thawed, melted, *resolved* into mist, "into a Dew," (that is, most particularly, non-"object"). Hamlet will become half ghost to himself. Later Ophelia, by drowning, mingling with water, will "Thaw" from her icy virginity to nonexistence. To thaw is to die, a metaphor for suicide, but suicide as an escape from the solid, threatening reality of the world. The Quarto's "too too sullied" was certainly a happy choice, for it spoke to Hamlet's sense of being tainted, soiled by his mother's marriage in his own flesh. Shakespeare revolving the line may have felt "sullied" smack of self-pity at so early a stage in the play. With a slight shift, the sentence served a deeper concern of the playwright. His "too too, solid" touches the opposition of nonbeing to being, so that "To be, or not to be" becomes a continuation of this "too too solid," of the Folio, a phrase that ushers in the Prince's descent to a world of death, ghosts, graves, suicide.

A characteristic of the Folio is its impatience with speech that is

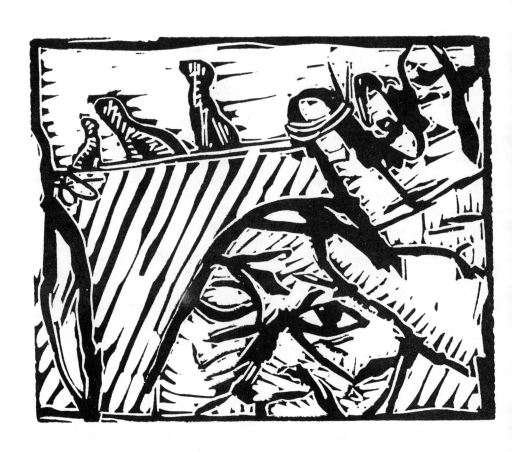

drawn out, artificially pretty or vaguely self-referential. The play-wright cut his own delays to preserve his Prince's. The longest Folio deletion early on is the Second Quarto soliloquy (and Bernardo's redundant speech introducing it) in which Horatio speaks of ghosts in Ancient Rome.

> *Ber.* I think it be no other, but enso;
> Well may it sort that this portentous figure
> Comes armed through our watch so like the King
> That was and is the question of these wars.
> *Hora.* A moth [mote] it is to trouble the mind's eye:
> In the most high and palmy state of Rome,
> A little ere the mightiest *Julius* fell
> The graves stood tenantless, and the sheeted dead
> Did squeak and gibber in the Roman streets
> As stars with trains of fire, and dews of blood
> Disasters in the sun; and the moist star,
> Upon whose influence *Neptunes* Empire stands,
> Was sick almost to doomesday with eclipse.
> And even the like precurse of feare [feared] events
> As harbingers preceding still the fates
> And prologue to the *Omen* coming on
> Have heaven and earth together demonstrated
> Unto our Climatures and countrymen.
>
> (Q2.B2ᵛ: 1.1.108–25)

The next major Folio excision is during the second scene on the battlements:

> This heavy headed revel east and west
> Makes us traduced, and taxed of other nations,
> They clip [call] us drunkards, and with Swinish phrase
> Soil our addition, and indeed it takes
> From our achievements, though perform'd at height
> The pith and marrow of our attribute,
> So oft it chances in particular men,
> That for some vicious mole of nature in them
> As in their birth wherein they are not guilty,
> (Since nature cannot choose his origin)
> By their ore-grow'th of some complexion
> Oft breaking down the pales and forts of reason,
> Or by some habit, that too much ore-leavens
> The form of plausive manners, that these men
> Carrying I say the stamp of one defect
> Being Natures livery, or Fortunes star,
> His virtues else be they as pure as grace,

As infinite as man may undergo,
Shall in the general censure take corruption
From that particular fault: the dram of eale [evil]
Doth all the noble substance of a doubt
To his own scandal.

(Q2.D-D^v:1.4.17–38)

(In his movie *Hamlet*, Olivier made these Quarto musings on "some vicious mole of nature," which would betray a man to "general censure," the epitomization of the Prince.[2])

Whether Hamlet, even unconsciously, is referring to himself, is doubtful. Why should Hamlet term *his* hesitation (which has not been demonstrated) a "vicious mole"? In the context of the country reels and drinking below, the obvious target is Claudius's drunkenness, the latter's pandering to a disposition for heavy drinking among the Danes. (Since Hamlet at the end of the battlement scenes will refer to the Ghost as an "old Mole," there may be some play of words in the playwright's mind between the Prince's father and uncle and their common danger to him, one as an underminer, the other as a malignant blemish.) The worst of the soliloquy is its "taint" of moralizing, which makes the Prince, priggish. Most of its message, though not its diction, could, if jingled into epigrams, be spoken by Polonius. In the Folio, the notion of "sullied" or "blemish" is no longer so important for Hamlet's flesh is not "too sullied" but rather "too solid." The exchange of flesh with the Ghost, the identification with the Ghost—not Gertrude—haunts the Folio's Shakespeare. Ophelia says, indirectly, that Hamlet, when he appears in her closet, looks like a ghost, and one who strangely resembles his own father "confin'd to fast in Fires," for the younger Hamlet "As if he had been loosed out of hell / To speak of horrors: he comes before me" (FF.2.1: 979–80). Hamlet has enacted before her the part of the Ghost, to hint by acting what has gone wrong. (Ophelia can not unfortunately interpret what she intuits until she has gone mad.)

It is his own reality that puzzles Hamlet, especially after his encounter with the Ghost. Two words added in the Folio to the text of the Quarto stress Shakespeare's concern through the Folio text with what is real, what imagined. In the soliloquy "O what a rogue and peasant slave am I," Hamlet builds to a frantic rant, after watching the players enact anger and grief. He piles on a catalogue of insults to prick himself to action against Claudius.

. . . for it cannot be
but I am pigeon livered, and lack gall

To make oppression bitter, or ere this
I should a fatted all the region kytes
With this slaves offal, bloody, bawdy villain,
Remorseless, treacherous, lecherous, kindless villain.
Why what an Ass am I, this is most brave,

(Q2.F4ᵛ-G: 2.2: 561–68)

The Folio changes the breath stop, by pausing after "bloody" and inserting the article "a," i.e., "a bawdy villain." The reason for this becomes apparent in a few seconds. For the summation of the rant is not the "villain" of the Quarto, but the cry, "O vengeance!"

With this Slaves Offal, bloody: **a** Bawdy villain,
Remorseless, Treacherous, Lecherous, kindless villain!
Oh Vengeance!
Who? What an Ass am I? **I sure,** this is most brave

(FF.2.2: 1620–23)

The drama of the speech lies in Hamlet's recoil from his own emotions, his distance, his suspicion of being manipulated by Hell. In the Quarto, it is his ranting against the villain Claudius that he suddenly pulls up short on and dismisses, going on to plot a definite action. In the Folio, however, it is Hamlet's own cry for "vengeance" that strikes him as asinine. This is an important shading for the Folio change calls the apparent motive of the play's actions, the revenge of a "dear [father] murdered," into question. Editors such as Farnham in the Pelican Shakespeare prefer the Quarto's "Why what an Ass . . . ?" The "Who?" in the Folio, however, is more mysterious, echoing down the long corridors of Elsinore. Who is calling for revenge—Hamlet or the Ghost? The "I sure," of the Folio stresses this mysterious "Who?" and assures the audience that they have heard correctly, Hamlet, turning on himself even as he questions himself. It is a double "I," for the "Who?" may be "I" or the Ghost, and who is the Ghost? Hamlet's sardonic "Prompted to my Revenge by Heaven, and Hell" fits the Folio's reading in a more intimate, suggestive fashion. "Who" is Hamlet calling to, "who" is calling to Hamlet?

* * *

Now enter Ophelia and the question in the flesh for Hamlet. Folio and Second Quarto again part radically. The Prince and Ophelia's exchange on Beauty and Honesty is sharpened. The set of oppositions, implicit in the questions "Are you honest?" and again "Are you fair?" muddied in the Quarto's "That if you be hon-

est & fair, you should admit / no discourse to your beauty," is kept
parallel in the Folio's: "That if you be honest and fair, **your Honesty** / should admit no discourse to your Beauty." It is Ophelia's
"Honesty" that Hamlet is harping on, and curiously this affects
Shakespeare's reworking of the imagery in which Hamlet de-
nounces "woman" before Ophelia. In the Second Quarto, the
prince cries:

> I have heard of your paintings well enough, God hath gi-
> ven you one face, and you make your selves another, you gig & am-
> ble, and you list you nickname Gods creatures, and make your wan-
> tonnes ignorance; go to, I'll no more on't, it hath made me mad.
>
> (Q2.G3: 3.1.142–46)

In the Folio, the metaphor of painting is replaced.

> I have heard of your **prattlings too** well enough.
> God has given you one **pace,** and you make **your self** an-
> other: you **gidge, you** amble, and you **lisp,** and nickname
> Gods creatures, and make your Wantonness, **your** Ig-
> norance. Go too, I'll no more on't, it hath made me mad.
>
> (FF.3.1: 1798–1802)

Shakespeare avoids the loaded word "painting" in the Folio
since he is not accusing Ophelia of being part of the counterfeit,
the painted scene, but rather of being stupid and using her sexual
arts to distract him from her "Ignorance." It is her lack of understanding that is making him "mad" not her participation in the
conspiracy. Ignorance has made her a pawn, just as her father and
brother will be, and she seems to Hamlet, especially dangerous.
(Directly after Hamlet's accusation, Polonius acquiesces in Hamlet's imprisonment: "Or confine him where / Your wisdom best
shall think." In this act, the counselor shows his ugly side. Polonius is no friend of Hamlet, as his position in Claudius's cabinet
indicates.) Ophelia's ignorance appears to Hamlet as a kind of
"Wantonness," an innocence so provocative it threatens to "blunt"
his purpose, to use the Ghost's rebuke. (Indeed the image of the
knife/phallus is the one Hamlet bandies with Ophelia in their last
exchange: "It would cost you a groaning, to take off my / edge"
[FF.3.2: 2117–18].)
    Why was it important for Shakespeare to keep Ophelia clear of
the conspiracy against Hamlet, even by implication—stressing this
in the Folio by changes and additions? The playwright, revising,
saw the Prince struggling against the Ghost, against the revenge.

Hamlet wants a normal life, a sexual life, and for this to be acted, Ophelia must remain relatively untainted (and so must Gertrude). In the short intervals of the drama he has arranged, Hamlet is seen in the Folio not jousting or insulting, but courting Ophelia. Their sexual play is an antiphony to the playlet of revenge. (The Folio's additions to the Quarto text are in boldface below, and I have followed its punctuation and capitalization)

Ham. Lady, shall I lie in your Lap?
Ophe. No my Lord.
Ham. **I mean, my Head upon your Lap?**
Ophe. **I my Lord.**
Ham. Do you think I meant Country matters?
Ophe. I think nothing, my Lord.
Ham. That's a faire thought to lie between Maids legs.
Ophe. What is my Lord?
Ham. Nothing.
Ophe. You are merry, my Lord? [Punctuated with . in the Quarto.]
Ham. Who I?
Ophe. I my Lord.
Ham. O God, your only Jigge-maker: what should
a man do but be merry for look you how cheerful-
ly my Mother looks, and my Father died within's two
Hours.
Oph. Nay, tis twice two months, my Lord.
(Q2H: 3.2.107–22 and FF 3.2: 1966–82)

The addition is meant to establish Hamlet's erotic fascination with Ophelia, his desire to signal her that he is still in love, that something *else* is wrong. It sharpens the erotic thrust of "shall I lie in your Lap" and yet wins from Ophelia consent to actually put his head in her lap, which he does in front of the whole court, a physical clarification.[3] The addition of the Second Quarto to the First Quarto, "That's a faire thought . . ." is brazen, a proposition of lust, which Hamlet must hope will draw an acknowledgement from Ophelia. She deliberately pretends she does not hear with, "What is, my Lord?" Then, and this is the actor's (or director's) choice, Hamlet either turns away with disgust, saying, "Nothing," or much more likely he mocks with it Ophelia's earlier "I think nothing," in response to his pointed, "Did you think I meant country matters?" The audience's attention to double meanings is alert here. Harold Jenkins notes in *The Arden Shakespeare*: "*Country matters:* physical lovemaking (with a popular pun on the first syllable)." Hamlet pauses, salaciously, midword, "Cunt-ry." In this context, Ophelia's unwitting "nothing," as Jenkins points out means vagina: "The absence of anything (in jocular allusion to virginity), perhaps with specific reference to the male 'thing.' Alternatively the figure 0, in allusion to the woman's sexual organ."[4] Ophelia, may rise naively to the bait of Hamlet's "That's a faire thought to lie between Maids legs," with "What is my Lord?" She is intended to get the joke when Hamlet repeats it. Her cheeks may redden, but it suggests a more sophisticated Ophelia, ready to challenge Hamlet a bit. This Ophelia is reflected in an earlier change in the Folio, when Hamlet denies giving her gifts and she uses "I": "I know right well you did," rather than the Second Quarto's, "you know right well you did."

There is no time for such an Ophelia to mature. Even in the Folio Ophelia is too timid, revenge too pressing. Hamlet tries to dally with his love, but Gertrude's betrayal is before him. He is dragged back to the play. So the Prince responds to Ophelia's half-hearted attempt to resume the sexual teasing "You are merry, my Lord" with a distracted reference to Gertrude, his father's death, and a confusion of time, "two Hours," against "twice two months." The speech does not end here, however, but goes on to the hobby horse: "a / great mans Memory, may out-live his life half a year: / But by [ou]rlady he must build Churches then: or else shall / he suffer not thinking on, with the Hoby-horse, whose / Epitaph is, For o, For o, the Hoby-horse is forgot" (FF.3.2: 1985–89). The "hoby horse" may well enact some of Hamlet's real confusion, which is not time but sex.

The speech has started with the language of the "jig" of woman's teasing: "O God, your only Jig-maker; what should / a man do, but be merry" (the "jig" previously twinned to Polonius's pleasure in "a tale of Bawdry" FF.2.2: 1540). At the end though, the hobby-horse refers explicitly to the dead king, Hamlet's father. The animal moves to the music of the jig. It is a mocking reference since the Ghost is being characterized as an actor's prop, and a ludicrous one, a horse's head on a stick serving to evoke between the legs of the morris dancer, the presence of the robust animal. It is a child's toy as well, and its position between the legs of the clown gives it a phallic connotation. Since Hamlet's head is in Ophelia's lap, he may well bounce up and down in a macabre image of the hobby horse who is forgotten, like his father's sexual power, by his mother, even as Prince Hamlet makes Ophelia feel his own presence with a "head" in her lap. It is funny, cruel, pathetic. The dumb show to follow enacts what we see before us between Hamlet and Ophelia, a king lying in a queen's lap. It goes a fatal step further, however, as the king falls asleep and murder peeps, the mise-en-scène another example of play within the play. The staging expresses the double play between Hamlet's love and his desire for revenge, his wish for Ophelia's sexual sympathy, his need to keep watch on Claudius. Juggling, the Prince answers Ophelia's question about whether the players will "tell us what this show meant?" with a reference to what he sees from her lap, i.e., her bosom.

Hamlet's frantic attempt to break through Ophelia's sexual naiveté is also his ploy to educate her about the situation in which he is caught. It is a plea for help, or at least sympathy. Thus the significance of the Folio's addition (in boldface) and changes. After the dumb show in the Second Quarto, as Ophelia says, "Belike this show imports the argument of the play," the stage direction reads, "Enter Prologue." Hamlet then refers to the Prologue in the singular: "We shall know by this fellow." In the Folio, the Prologue does not enter until his lines several moments later. Thus he does not distract Ophelia from the import of Hamlet's warning:

We shall know by these Fellows: the Players
cannot keep **counsel,** they'll tell all.
Ophe. Will they tell us what this show meant?
Ham. I, or any show that you'll show him. Be not
you asham'd to show, he'll not shame to tell you what it
means.
Ophe. You are naught, you are naught, I'll mark the
Play.
Enter Prologue.

(FF.3.2: 2008–15)

Under these lines, accompanied by his naked, provocative stare up at her breasts from Ophelia's lap, which the later remark "I could interpret between you and your love: / if I could see the Puppets dallying" (FF.3.2: 2114–15) can be taken to refer to as well (the "poopies" of the First Quarto, having become "puppets")[5] runs Hamlet's cry to Ophelia: "Be not / you asham'd to show." If she gives him her body, he will trust her with his "counsel," and "not shame to tell you what it / means," i.e., the dumb show. Her response is a coy reproof: "You are naught, you are naught," and "I'll mark the / Play." This pretense to prefer the play to the Prince, which is followed by a particularly superficial piece of poetry, the short doggerel of the player's introduction, draws from Hamlet a cry of despair at breaking through to this "green girl." In reply to Ophelia's defense of the Prologue, "'Tis brief my Lord," Hamlet mutters—speaking in the same breath of the Player-Queen in the play, Gertrude, and Ophelia—"As Woman's love." The sardonic epigram is also, alas, an appeal.

The "Mousetrap" or "Murder of Gonzago" is tightened considerably in the Folio.[6] Its wordy speeches, which make the action unwieldy, are cut down to tolerable length; three lines go in one of Baptista's speeches, two lines in another, and so space is given for the expansion of the erotic dialogue between Hamlet and Ophelia. Interrupting Hamlet's dialogue with the King, Ophelia jibes, "You are a good Chorus, my Lord" (*FF.* 3.2: 2113), trying to pull the Prince back into her orbit. This is daring of her, and Hamlet does return to pay suit, teasing her about a lover (and possibly her "breasts," which may be the "puppets dallying.") When Ophelia cries in good humor, "You are keen my Lord, you are keen," Hamlet goes on to her virginity: "It would cost you a groaning, to take off my / edge." This time Ophelia does not avoid the dialogue that she had previously when he faced her with "that's a faire thought to lie between maids legs," but rather, answers saucily, "Still better and worse."[7] Rolling the next line's "miss-take" on the tongue makes the pun of Hamlet's answer obvious. "So you mistake Husbands" (*FF.*3.2: 2120). "Must take" and "mis-take" are close to the ear, and the line before is the familiar wedding pledge, to take a mate "For better and for worse." The Folio "mis-take," cutting the Quarto's "your" is the reading preferred. "So you mistake **your** husbands," reads the Second Quarto. A "your" generalizes the remark. The epigram in the Folio refers to Ophelia's doubt that Hamlet intends to marry her, to the question of fidelity, of loyalty between husband and wife. Heard as "mistake," it refers to Gertrude, as well as Ophelia, for it means *so* you take a husband, *badly* and are mistaken in your choice. Heard, however, as "must take," it implies you must take a husband for his evil as well as his good, *and* you must *satisfy* a husband in the body as well as the mind. Even understood as "mistake" meaning "misunderstand," however, there is a sexual rebuke in the Prince's rejoinder as if he is chiding Ophelia for alluding to his desire for her "groaning," or surrender as "worse."

From his dialogue with Ophelia Hamlet jumps back to the play before them, "The Mousetrap," the drama of a "mis-take," with his cry, "Begin Murderer." That "worse," though, sticks. It is the final exchange between Hamlet and Ophelia, her last word to him, and it is a rejection of his demand for an erotic understanding. The confidence of this sexual bond, which Gertrude has betrayed in Hamlet's imagination, is mirrored in the "mis-take." In the "give and take" between Ophelia and Hamlet, the girl will take his wit, but not give her body in return, "take off" his "edge." Still Ophelia is high-spirited at this moment, making her descent into madness more awful. "The time is out of joint": in this play of delay, there is no time for Ophelia to develop into the woman Hamlet needs.

Revising, Shakespeare has Hamlet struggling harder, despite his revenge and its suicidal nature, to hold on to Ophelia whom he can and does love, although she is no help to him. Hamlet has only Horatio and his mother. (Although Hamlet's inability to trust Gertrude is part of his downfall.) He does "taint" his "mind" against her, contrary to the Ghost's instructions and loses valuable time. Ophelia, in madness, will ultimately be loyal to Hamlet, denouncing Claudius before her brother as "the false Steward that stole his masters daughter" (FF.4.5; 2925).[8] (All the riddling lines in Ophelia's mad scenes are cryptograms in the spirit of Hamlet's earlier ones, "Fishmonger," etc.) In a politically deft announcement at the beginning of the play that Hamlet is to succeed to the throne, Claudius makes himself "steward" or guardian of the royal line. This unriddles the "masters daughter," for Ophelia is not referring to Polonius, but her hope once to be daughter-in-law to the dead king. Claudius has betrayed Ophelia in murdering and plotting murder. (Likewise in the language of indirection, Ophelia bewails her refusal to give her body, the "bread" in the folk tale about the Baker's daughter who would not feed Jesus, to Hamlet.[9] (The identification between bread and body, a mystery of the Catholic sacrament, points the sacrilegious anger of Ophelia. For her erotic refusal Ophelia sings; she has been turned like the Baker's daughter into an owl, an emblem of mourning and wisdom.) As she exits Ophelia signals danger to Laertes from Claudius through the language of flowers by giving the king a daisy, symbol of dissimulation. But Laertes is unable to "reason" his sister's madness, just as Ophelia was unable to reason Hamlet's until her father's death brought her into the grip of the irrational. Such is the comment of the playwright on "reason." To "reason" however, in a moment.

*   *   *

The next significant Folio revisions are seen as Ophelia rises and Claudius flees.[10] Shakespeare sets himself to alter Gertrude in the Folio dampening the violence of Hamlet's Second Quarto accusations:

Ger. Come, come, you answer with an idle tongue.
Ham. Go, go, you question with a wicked tongue.

In the Folio, Hamlet doesn't characterize Gertrude's tongue as "wicked," but only returns her adjective, "idle."

Ger. Come, come, you answer with an idle tongue.
Ham. Go, go, you question with **an idle** tongue.

This throws the emphasis on "question" and points his mother's refusal to be direct with him in her questions. In the Second Quarto, Hamlet seems to object to being Gertrude's son. The Folio changes make clear it is the marriage to Claudius that the Prince regrets. This gives Hamlet's "You are my Mother," a few lines on in the scene, a new pathos. Rubbing away some of Hamlet's harshness emphasizes his admission of love, the playwright's desire to cast Gertrude in a more sympathetic, therefore ambiguous, role. In the Second Quarto, Hamlet rails of the "act" she has committed, that it

. . . takes of the Rose
From the fair forehead of an innocent love,
And sets a blister there . . . .

(Q2.I2ᵛ: 3.4.43–45)

The Folio **"makes"** is less forceful than "sets a blister there." The latter suggests the brand "set" in the forehead of a whore.

takes off the Rose
From the fair forehead of an innocent love,
And **makes** a blister there

(FF.3.4: 2425–27)

Hamlet speaks of Heaven in the Quarto as having a "heated visage," but the Folio has a gentler, "tristful visage."

. . . heaven's face does glow
Ore this solidity and compound mass
With heated visage, as against the doom
Is thought sick at the act
Quee. Ay me, what act?
Ham. That roars so loud, and thunders in the Index.

(Q2.I2ᵛ:3.4.49–53)

. . . Heaven's face doth glow,
Yea this solidity and compound mass,
With **tristful** visage as against the doom,
Is thought-sick at the act.
Qu. Aye me; what act, that roars so loud, & thun-
ders in the Index.

(FF.3.4: 2431–36)

Consonant with his previous corrections, Shakespeare shifts
Hamlet's Second Quarto lines "That roars so loud, and thunders
in the Index," to Gertrude in the Folio. The cry, bombast in the
Prince's mouth, is more appropriate as part of Gertrude's protest
against his moral vehemence. Gertrude's demand that her son clarify "what act" is the crux of the Folio revision. Will Hamlet repeat
the accusation twice made as he took his bloody dagger from Polonius—that his mother knew her husband was murdered? In neither Folio or Second Quarto does Hamlet reply to her demand
"Aye me, what act?" in neither play does Gertrude start with guilt,
despite the deceptive, "Aye me," which seems to promise a confession. Neither version charges her with murder, but the Second
Quarto rushes by her denial and her plea. In both, Hamlet realizes
that it is only copulation he can charge her with, incest, and that
sounds too crude as an answer to "what act?" Hamlet must work
on his mother's guilt, and this requires a device, which is what the
portraits around their necks provide. The Second Quarto's Hamlet
jumps from bombast to portrait. In the Folio, Gertrude silences
Hamlet. There is a pause when he realizes his mistake earlier. "As
kill a King?" Gertrude asks. "I Lady, 'twas my word," Hamlet answers, but obviously does not see in her the start of guilt he just
had from Claudius. In the Folio's shift of the reprimand, "that roars
so loud," the audience and Hamlet are given a moment in which
to understand Gertrude's innocence of murder. (This is part of the
larger revision Shakespeare is making in Gertrude's character.)
Hamlet, in the Folio, pauses after Gertrude's reprimand. He takes
up the portrait around his neck, deliberately, as a more appropriate way of speaking his disgust at her embrace in the "act" now
understood as solely the copulative "act" with Claudius. Shakespeare cut ten lines from the Second Quarto (indicated below in
boldface) that are nerveless, abstract, talking about sense and motion. The play concentrates its denunciation, going more directly
to Gertrude's question, "what act?" Hamlet answers with "O
Shame! where is thy Blush? . . . canst mutiny in a Matron's bones
. . . Proclaim no shame . . . ." This indeed has the desired effect

on Gertrude and brings on the tears Hamlet has been hoping for, the repentance (lines unique to Second Quarto are in boldface):

> . . . and what judgment[11]
> Would step from this to this, **sense sure you have**
> **Else could you not have motion, but sure that sense**
> **Is apoplext, for madness would not err**
> **Nor sense to ecstasy was near so thral'd**
> **But it reserved some quantity of choice**
> **To serve in such a difference,** what devil wast
> That thus hath cozened you at hoodman blind;
> **Eyes without feeling, feeling without sight,**
> **Ears without hands, or eyes, smelling sans all,**
> **Or but a sickly part of one true sense**
> **Could not so mope:** o shame where is thy blush?
> Rebellious hell,
> If thou canst mutiny in a Matrons bones,
> To flaming youth let virtue be as wax
> And melt in her own fire, proclaim no shame
> When the compulsive ardor gives the charge,
> Since frost itself as actively doth burn,
> And reason pardons will.
>
> (Q2.I3: 3.4.71–89)

Later on, when Gertrude begins to weep rather than protest, Hamlet will refer to the "the rank sweat of an enseamed bed, / Stew'd in Corruption; honying and making love / Over the nasty Sty" (F.F.3.4: 2469–71). Here Gertrude will cry out to stop her son from describing the act of copulation, "speak . . . no more," wrung from her a second time. The third "No more" comes just as Hamlet seems about to give details of Claudius's role in his brother's murder. This brings in the Ghost, whether to protect Gertrude or to stop Hamlet from revealing the Ghost's role and his knowledge is deliberately ambiguous.

The soliloquy previous is the one place in the Folio where Shakespeare sharpens the denunciation: "reason" does not as in the Quarto, "pardon will." In the Folio, "Reason **panders** Will." The attack on reason goes on all through *Hamlet,* and it is quickened in the Folio by the cuts. Reason, which would deny the Ghost, is the sovereign weapon of Claudius. Reason is heard even more maliciously twisted in the mouths of Rosencrantz and Guildenstern. Hamlet has to appeal continually to intuition. The attack on reason, however, threatens Hamlet and is in part responsible for his vertigo. Ophelia realizes this, although her own reason is extremely fragile. The line of the Ghost about Gertrude could apply equally to Ophelia: "Conceit in weakest bodies, strongest works."

Hamlet himself is vulnerable in this scene. (Olivier, in his cinematic staging, chose to have the Prince faint before the appearance of the Ghost in Gertrude's chamber.) Gertrude says of her handsome son here, in repugnant horror, "Your bedded hair, like life in excrements, / Start up, and stand an [on] end." Hamlet looks like a creature of the grave to her, his hair a breeder of maggots. That Hamlet sees the Ghost, but Gertrude does not, evokes pathos and vertigo. The audience remembers from the scenes on the battlements that the Ghost *is* real. Now the Ghost's reality is questioned, and the audience, at the edge of the invisible, must wonder at its own credibility. Hamlet, seeing that his mother can not see, is face to face with his own strangeness. He (and we, the audience) are in another world. Hamlet himself speaks of tears overwhelming him at the sight of the Ghost, whom he first asks the angels to defend him from:

> . . . Do not look upon me,
> Least with this piteous action you convert
> My stern effects: then what I have to do,
> Will want true color; tears perchance for blood.
>
> (*FF.*3.4: 2508–11)

This is the very melting, the Prince had hoped for, thawing into tears, death at the play's beginning. Hamlet fears it now ostensibly because it will make revenge impossible, but it expresses a new disgust both towards the Ghost and the ghostly. Sight of the dead father does not stiffen Hamlet's resolve or "whet" his "almost blunted purpose," but rather dissolves it. The Folio enforces this vulnerability—its Prince is too shaken to go on about the "monster custom." If anything convinces that Shakespeare's hand might be at work on the revision, it is the following cut (Second Quarto in boldface).

> Assume a virtue if you have it not,
> **That monster custom, who all sense doth eat**
> **Of habits devil, is angel yet in this**
> **That to the use of actions fair and good,**
> **He likewise gives a frock or Livery**
> **That aptly is put on to** refrain night, [to night in *FF.*]
> And that shall lend a kind of easiness
> To the next abstinence, **the next more easy:**
> **For use almost can change the stamp of nature,**

And either the devil, or throw him out
With wondrous potency: once more good night,

(Q2.I4: 3.4.161–71)

The Quarto's version is wordy, sententious. The Folio cuts to the message half-buried in pompous phrase, delivers it, and bids the Queen good night.

The Folio also cuts a redundant "One word more good Lady" in the last moments of the scene, and changes "the blowt King," which suggests both the swollen infected flesh of Claudius and his flabbiness, to "the blunt King." The latter seems to be a sarcastic reference to Claudius's sexual clumsiness in line with the "take off my / edge," remark (FF.3.2: 2117–18) Hamlet has made to Ophelia. In the Second Quarto, Hamlet reflects upon the sealed letters, the treachery of his two schoolfellows and his intention to betray them. This, cut in the Folio, leaves both what he knows and the Queen knows more ambiguous. (Q2. in boldface.)

> *Ham.* I must to England, you know that?
> *Ger.* Alack I had forgot: 'Tis so concluded on.
> *Ham.* **Theres letters sealed, and my two Schoolfellows,**
> **Whom I will trust as I will Adders fang'd,**
> **They bear the mandate, they must sweep my way**
> **And marshal me to knavery: let it work,**
> **For tis the sport to have the engineer**
> **Hoist with his own petar, an't shall go hard**
> **But I will delve one yard below their mines,**
> **And blow them at the Moon: o tis most sweet**
> **When in one line two crafts directly meet,**
> This man shall set me packing:

(Q2.I4ᵛ-K: 3.4.201–12)

In the scene that follows, Gertrude, for the first time, stands up to the King, says that Hamlet, whose "madness . . . Shows itself pure," is weeping for his deed, a lie that gives proof of her shift of sympathies. Claudius must feel this for he instantly changes his tune, with "O *Gertrude*, come away." (In the Folio, Claudius is "my good Lord" (FF.4.1: 2591) not "mine own Lord" [Q2.K: 4.1.5].) The entrance of Hamlet after the King exits, the Gentlemen calling for the Prince interspersed with the Prince's lines, is more skillful.[12] The Second Quarto speaks of the courtier as an "apple" in the jaw of the King. The apple is cut from the Folio and instead the King is seen as a chewing "Ape," which repeats the image of the foolish ape in Hamlet's speech a few moments before to Gertrude. In both

speeches, Hamlet is prophesying the downfall of those who col-
laborate with Claudius as well as Claudius.[13] This animal imagery
is extended in the Folio addition, "hide Fox, and all / after" (FF.4.2:
2659–60), which sounds like the exit of Lear where the courtiers
chase the demented monarch. The line added to the Folio gives an
antic madness to Hamlet. It points the rapid whirling around of
Hamlet and the King on the stage not by coincidence but by pres-
sure of the action.

When Hamlet leaves the stage for England, the Folio works in
the Prince's absence to strengthen Gertrude. It drops the Quarto's
gentleman in act 4, scene 5, transferring to Horatio and Gertrude
lines about the dangers of Ophelia's mutterings. Gertrude, therefore, appears to be acting in concert with Horatio. The effect is to
present her as allied to Hamlet's party, as opposed to Claudius's.
While it is never clear how much Gertrude knows (like Ophelia),
the Folio indicates more of a change in Gertrude after her bedroom
conversation with Hamlet. In both Folio and Second Quarto, Gertrude thrusts herself between Laertes and Claudius to protect the
latter, or seem to.

> *Laer.* Where's my Father?
> *King.* Dead.
> *Qu.* But not by him.
>
> (FF.4.5: 2873–75)

Can the Queen be referring to Hamlet with her ambiguous "him"?
Gertrude's consorting with Horatio strengthens the suspicion that
at the critical moment she drinks the poison to protect her son. In
the Folio it is Gertrude not Horatio who calls in Ophelia to stop
her roaming about, upsetting the populace.

> 'Twere good she were spoken with,
> For she may strew dangerous conjectures
> In ill breeding minds. Let her come in.
>
> (FF.4.5: 2759–61)

Gertrude is guarding her son's kingdom and beginning to rule.
The Quarto deprives her of this forethought and self-assurance.
(Horatio maintains his initiative in the Folio through the lines
transferred to him here from the Quarto's gentleman.)

In discussing Shakespeare's "cast of Thought" at the moment
of revising the Second Quarto, the lines of the First Quarto of 1603
provide an intriguing perspective. If the 1603 Quarto is indeed

Shakespeare's first text of *Hamlet*, his early Gertrude had a very different role to play than his later Queens.

> One of the largest-scale distinctions in the multiple texts of *Hamlet* changes the conception of the role of the Queen. The ambiguous, troubled woman we know in the Second Quarto and Folio texts is deeply in love with her present husband, and she is deeply troubled by the wild eruptions of rage she witnesses in her son. But . . . the Queen does not learn of the assaults made by the King upon her first husband and upon her son. . . . In sharp contrast, the character of the Queen given in the First Quarto learns early of the King's crimes, and she enlists herself in Hamlet's aid. In the Closet Scene, 3.4, in this earliest extant version of the play, Hamlet directly names Claudius as a murderer, *and*, unlike the equivalent passage in the Second Quarto and the Folio, he names his father as Claudius' victim.

> > A! have you eyes and can you looke on him
> > That slew my father, and your deere husband,
> > To live in the incestuous pleasure of his bed?

> In lines found only in the First Quarto, the Queen replies to Hamlet's revelation.

> > But as I have a soule, I sweare by heaven
> > I never knew of this most horride murder:

> Hamlet asks her to join him in revenge, and she agrees . . . . Later, in a scene found only in the First Quarto, the Queen learns from Horatio of the King's plot to have Hamlet killed in England. . . . She sends Horatio to Hamlet with words of caution and with her blessings. These and other details of action in the First Quarto are consistent with the Queen being an active ally of Hamlet, knowledgeable about the risks he faces.[14]

Did the Shakespeare of the Folio feel he had gone too far in making Gertrude ambiguous, that she had lost sympathy from her son—and for her son? If the First Quarto is an early draft, one may trace Shakespeare's movement from simple to complex motivation. Removing the empathy of son and mother, the Second Quarto marred an earlier complexity. Were the revisions of the Folio to adjust the Second Quarto's? Sympathy for Gertrude is essential to an audience's concern for her son, Hamlet. The agony of the Queen almost knowing or suspecting, raising the poisoned cup in the last act not in ignorance but with the intuition of horror, is indicated by the Folio's reversion after the revision of the Second Quarto, to a shadow of the First Quarto of 1603, Gertrude aware.[15]

The First Quarto may have influenced another set of changes in the Folio. The Second Quarto not only expanded the scene between Laertes and Claudius as they plot to murder Hamlet, it revised the character of Polonius's son.

> In a second major plot-variation, the plan of Laertes and the King to murder Hamlet develops differently in the First Quarto from the Second Quarto and Folio. The King in Q1 tells Laertes every aspect of the proposed duelling accident. The King suggests all three parts of the treacherous scheme, first the unbaited sword, then the poisoned blade, and finally the poisoned drink. . . . A further set of linked variants shows us the King's mind at work in Q2-F with a kind of demonic inventiveness—"Let's further thinke of this, . . . soft, let me see . . . I hate" [i.e. "I ha't" or "I have it!"] an alacrity of evil spirit not realized in the First Quarto."[16]

The scene in the Second Quarto, however, goes on at length and may have played badly. Did Shakespeare in his Folio revision, remember the taut line of action in the First Quarto? From the Folio he cut dialogue, added in the Second Quarto, where Laertes volunteers himself as the instrument not of revenge but treachery. These sixteen lines were excised.

> *Laer.* My Lord I will be rul'd,
> The rather if you could devise it so
> That I might be the organ.
> *King.* It falls right,
> You have been talked of since your travel much,
> And that in *Hamlets* hearing, for a quality
> Wherein they say you shine, your sum of parts
> Did not together pluck such envy from him
> As did that one, and that in my regard
> Of the unworthiest siege.
> *Laer.* What part is that my Lord?
> *King.* A very riband in the cap of youth,
> Yet needful too, for youth no less becomes
> The light and careless livery that it wears
> Than settled age, his sables, and his weedes
> Importing health and graveness;
>
> (Q2.L4: 4.7.67–80)

Self-conscious poetry, a bit too pretty at the end, the Second Quarto lines weaken the sense of Claudius's resolve and make

Laertes too willfully set on the murder. Talk of Hamlet's envy is redundant, for a few lines on Claudius will mention that the report of Laertes's skill with the rapier: "Did *Hamlet* so envenom with his envy, / That he could nothing do but wish and beg, / Your sudden coming ore to play with you:" (Q2.L4ᵛ: 4.7.102–4). Just before this, Shakespeare cut from the Folio another three redundant lines, praising Laertes:

> . . . the Scrimatures of their nation
> He swore had neither motion, guard, nor eye,
> If you opposed them;
>
> (Q2.L4ᵛ: 4.7.99–101)

Claudius is getting too wrapped up in his description and losing his main point—are you ready for murder? emphasized by the Folio, which cuts to the essential:

> *Laertes* was your father dear to you?
> Or are you like the painting of a sorrow,
> A face without a heart?
>
> (Q2.L4ᵛ: 4.7.106–8)

Claudius's use of the language of painting, which signifies the decorative exterior of emotion, is apt. A complex image in *Hamlet*, paint may conceal evil, or as Claudius knows, emptiness.[17] In the Second Quarto, Shakespeare let Claudius's disposition to "paint" words get out of hand. The Folio cuts yet another ten Quarto lines from this scene where Claudius waxes philosophical and begins to sound like Hamlet.

> There lives within the very flame of love
> A kind of wick or snuff that will abate it,
> And nothing is at a like goodness still,
> For goodness growing to a pleurisy,
> Dies in his own too much, that we would do
> We should do when we would: for this would changes,
> And hath abatements and delays as many,
> As there are tongues, are hands, are accidents,
> And then this should is like a spend thrifts sigh,
> That hurts by easing; but to the quick of th'ulcer,
>
> (Q2.L4ᵛ: 4.7.113–22)

There is no need to stir Laertes to action, he is already prepared.

* * *

At the very end of *Hamlet*, the Folio makes several surprising additions and changes to the Second Quarto (indicated in bold-face). The lines added more than make up for the tedious ones cut. In the first Folio addition, the sexual laughter of Hamlet, dismissing the clumsy villainy of his old schoolfellows is heard:

Hor. So *Guildenstern and Rosincranz*, go too't.
Ham. Why man, they did make love to this employment
They are not near my Conscience; their [defeat Q2] **debate**
Doth by their own insinuation grow:

(*FF.*5.2: 3559–62)

The sexual pun of Horatio, "go too't," as a synonym for vigorous and joyful copulation, is an indication of more mettle than one might have suspected. Horatio's grim joke is about surrendering not one's organ to sex, but one's head to the axe, i.e., being murdered. (Dying and coming to orgasm are synonyms in Elizabethan usage.) In the Second Quarto, Hamlet uncharacteristically ignores Horatio's pun, but, in the Folio, he wittily tops it, referring not only to their death, but what brought them to it, as a form of erotic joy. "Why man, they did make love to this employment!": this is macabre but exquisite humor, the "grave" humor which is the very essence of the play.

The jesting transforms Claudius's sententious word play at the very beginning, where life and death were posed as opposites and language sought to conceal the King's treachery. In the graveyard, Hamlet truly sees the "mirth in Funeral." The wisdom of Claudius was wholly conventional, poisonously so, like Polonius's. Life and death, delight and dole, seen as bifurcated.

Th'Imperiall Jointress of this warlike State,
Have we, as 'twere, with a defeated joy,
With one Auspicious, and one Dropping eye,
With mirth in Funeral, and with Dirge in Marriage,
In equal Scale weighing Delight and Dole
Taken to Wife;

(*FF.*1.2: 187–92)

Rosencrantz and Guildenstern face a "defeated joy," in truth, an axe the consummation of their murderous employment, an unexpected, "Dirge in Marriage." Hamlet having wrestled with the Ghost, his father, with his own will to live, with his erotic life and Ophelia, can say now to his own anxiety, "If it be now, 'tis not / to come" (*FF.*5.2: 3669–70). The anxiety of what will come, "what dreams may come," is still greater than the fear of the moment. Yet "now" all is irony. With a certain flippancy—"we defy Augury"— Hamlet prepares himself for the fencing match. He jokes to Horatio: "since no / man ha's ought of what he leaves. What is't to leave be- / times?" (*FF*.5.2: 3671–73). At the moment of death, however, Hamlet will fear for the name he leaves behind and for the kingdom. He will order Horatio not to leave him with "a wounded name," but to report the "Story." (It seems as if Shakespeare has anticipated the epigram in Milton's "Lycidas": "*Fame* is the spur that the clear spirit doth raise / (That last infirmity of Noble mind)." Fame is the poet's occupational infirmity, not necessarily the Prince's.)

With bloodthirsty joking about Rosencrantz & Guildenstern, then, in a cry for action, the Hamlet of the Folio additions (boldface below) anticipates the fight that looms. In the Second Quarto, Hamlet's pledge is cut off before it can be concluded, by the entrance of the courtier, Osric (appropriately) on the word "conscience."

Does it not, thinkst thee, stand me now upon
He that hath kill'd my King, and whor'd my Mother,
Popt in between th'election and my hopes,
Thrown out his Angle for my proper life,
And with such cozenage; is't not perfect conscience,
To quit him with this arm? And is't not to be damn'd
To let this Canker of our nature come
In further evil.
Hor. **It must be shortly known to him from England**
What is the issue of the business there.
Ham. **It will be short,**
The *interim's* **mine, and a mans life's no more**
The[a]n to say one: but I am very sorry good *Horatio,*
That to *Laertes* **I forgot my self;**
For by the image of my Cause, I see
The Portraiture of his; Ile coun[r]t his favors:
But sure the bravery of his grief did put me
Into a Towering passion.

                                             (*FF*.5.2: 3567–84)

Here the "vicious mole" cut from act 1, scene 4 reappears as a "Canker of our nature," and to let it remain is to be "damn'd" though the surgery be fatal since it is strangely self-referential. The end is looming, days aways, perhaps hours, Horatio warns his friend in the Folio: "It must be shortly known to him from England / What is the issue of the business there." Shakespeare is alerting the audience to the peril of Hamlet's *"interim."* The deaths of the two emissaries soon to be known, Hamlet must act immediately. Hamlet aware of this, *has no plans*! This is the perversity (or saintliness) of the Prince's character. Then there are fatal lines in which he uses the language of Claudius in speaking of Laertes's "Portraiture" and falls into the counterfeiters' trap. Laertes has falsified reality. Something of that understanding lingers in Hamlet's musing on Laertes's melodramatic rage in the graveyard, its "bravery," or overemphasis, which masks emptiness and guilt.

Hamlet pauses, speaking of action, but not plotting, holding himself but in "readiness." Shakespeare in the Folio, however cuts,[18] cuts, to hurry the resolution on so that the terrible approach of the event may be felt. The playwright slashes the scene with Osric, omits the whole tedious Second Quarto description of Laertes's coming to court (boldface below):

. . . here is newly
come to Court *Laertes,* **believe me an absolute gentlemen, full of most excellent differences, of very soft society, and great showing: indeed to speak feelingly of him, he is the card or calender of gentry: for you shall find in him the continent of what part a Gentleman would see.**
Ham. **Sir, his definement suffers no perdition in you, though I know to divide him inventorially, would dazzle th'arithmetic of memory, and yet but raw neither, in respect of his quick sail, but in the verity of extolment, I take him to be a soul of great article, & his infusion of such dearth and rareness, as to make true diction of him, his semblable is his mirror, & who else would trace him, his umbrage, nothing more.**
Cour. **Your Lordship speaks most infallibly of him.**
Ham. **The concernancy sir, why do we wrap the gentleman in our more rawer breath?**
Cour. **Sir.**
Hor. **Ist not possible to understand in another tongue, you will do't sir really.**
Ham. **What imports the nomination of this gentleman.**
Cour. **Of** *Laertes.*
Hor. **His purse is empty already, all's golden words are spent.**
Ham. **Of him sir.**
Cour. **I know you are not ignorant.**
Ham. **I would you did sir, yet in faith if you did, it would not much approve me, well sir.**

(Q2.N2–N2^v: 5.2.106–33)

The lines that follow:

> *Cour.* **You are not ignorant of what excellence *Laertes* is.**
> *Ham.* **I dare not confess that, least I should compare with**
> **him in excellence, but to know a man well, were to know himself.**
> *Cour.* **I mean sir for this weapon, but in the imputation laid on**
> **him, by them in his meed, he's unfellowed.**
>
> (Q2.N2ᵛ: 5.2.134–39)

are boiled down in the Folio to one remark of Osric's: "Sir, you are not ignorant of what excellence *Laertes* is at / his weapon." (*FF*.5.2: 3611–12). Horatio's rather lame, **"I knew you must be edified by the margent ere you had / done"** (Q2.N2ᵛ: 5.2.150–51), is deleted. The drawn out back and forth between Osric and Hamlet, the latter mocking the former's language, is comedy too relaxed for the moment. The entrance of a second Lord in the Second Quarto to remind Hamlet of his pledge to duel delays the action further. The Folio cuts it; likewise Gertrude's instruction to **"use some gentle entertainment / to *Laertes*"** (Q2.N3ᵛ) and the announcement that the King and Queen are coming, which adds nothing to the tension of the clock ticking away; all chopped out in the Folio's momentum.

In the Folio, news from England imminent, Hamlet feels this. Hamlet's apprehension is what is most important. To that Shakespeare goes immediately in the Folio, the ominous line of Horatio, with its addition of **"this wager."** Does Hamlet in the line "we defy Augury" in fact defy the warning of the Ghost? The Prince has been warned by the "kind of gain-giving" about his heart. The very vagueness of the warning makes Shakespeare, revising, eager to clarify.

> *Hor.* You will lose my Lord.
>
> (Q2.N3ᵛ: 5.2.198)
>
> *Hor.* You will lose **this wager,** my Lord.
>
> (*FF*.5.2: 3658)
>
> *Ham.* . . . if it be, tis not to come,
>
> (Q2.N3ᵛ: 5.2.209)
>
> *Ham.* If it be **now,** 'tis not
> to come:
>
> (*FF*.5.2: 3669–70)

These seem to make the meaning of the lines clearer. The slight change in the final lines of 5.2, however, embraces a world of difference.

since no man **of** ought he leaves, **knows** what ist to leave betimes, **let be.**

(Q2.N3^v: 5.2.211–12)

. . . since no
man **ha's** ought of **what** he leaves. What is't to leave betimes?

(FF.5.2: 3671–73)

Hamlet in the Quarto appears to speak of man not knowing anything of what he leaves behind when he dies. Therefore he laughs at Horatio, what is the difference between leaving early or late.[19] This indicates an afterworld to which the present world means nothing, a vision contradicted by the whole force of the revenge tragedy. The Folio's Hamlet speaks of man in the afterworld, unable to have anything that he has left in the present. Therefore it is a matter of indifference whether one dies early. This certainly refers to Hamlet's ambition to hold the throne and indirectly to the sadness of the Ghost, forced to leave his wife and son behind. In this sense, it speaks both the melancholy of the play and the threat of the ghostly, as the dead father moils in anger, under the stage.

The most important of these minor Folio additions occurs as Hamlet addresses the circle of the court gathered to witness the duel. The Folio's "**Sir, in this Audience**" (FF.5.2: 3692) before the line "Let my disclaiming from a purpos'd evil" clarifies the judicial function of the court audience. The Folio's addition underlines the strategy of Shakespeare's conclusion. The King will be proved a poisoner and murderer in front of the court of Denmark. This is not a trivial change or addition for it witnesses the judicial assent of the royal court to Claudius's execution by his nephew.

One of the most peculiar differences between Folio and Quarto is Hamlet's use of the word "Mother" rather than "Brother" in his speech of reconciliation with Laertes.

Sir, in this Audience,
Let my disclaiming from a purpos'd evil,
Free me so far in your most generous thoughts,
That I have shot mine Arrow o're the house,
And hurt my **Mother.**

(FF.5.2: 3692–96)

Is it merely a printer's mistake? The audience has been warned by Hamlet's earlier farewell to Claudius, "Farewell dear Mother," to listen for this catch. The Prince, with an amusement that is angry, almost perverse, turns the conventional phrase. Hamlet has indeed meant in stabbing through the arras to murder his father/ mother, Claudius. The court now may well murmur and pause at the strange substitution, and Laertes, in the silence, decide to pretend that he is satisfied in "nature." The word "brother" is used by Hamlet further on: "I do embrace it freely, / And will this Brothers wager frankly play" (FF.5.2: 3706–7). All these words are "loaded" and fraught with double meaning. Laertes has replied to Hamlet, "I do receive your offer'd love like love, / And will not wrong it" (FF.5.2: 3704–5), which is rhetorical double-talk. Given the treachery of Claudius to his brother, Hamlet's "Brothers wager," has an ominous sound. The Prince's vigorous, **"Come on,"** added in the Folio, emphasizes his cheerful sarcasm. Laertes protests, "You mock me Sir" (FF.5.2: 3713), and this seems to confirm Hamlet's intentional use of "Mother" just before.

The Folio adds a stage direction *Prepare to play* (FF.5.2: 3725) just as Hamlet says to Osric, "These Foils have all a length." The direction indicates that Hamlet and Osric are together, taking up positions for the match when the King's speech interrupts them. Osric's answer—"I my good Lord" suggests that while Claudius distracts the Prince, Osric, and the court, Laertes juggles a foil in his hand so as to anoint it, perhaps bends it from the tip, as if to weigh its bulk by the measure of its bend. Osric seems too great a fool, like Polonius, to be part of the plotting (as the role is played in the Olivier *Hamlet*). Hamlet's previous lines about Osric indicate that he is at court not because he is a courtier, but because "he hath much Land, and fertile; let a Beast / be Lord of Beasts, and his Crib shall stand at the Kings / Mess; 'tis a Chough; but as I saw spacious in the pos- / session of dirt" (FF.5.2: 3591–94). (Later he is referred to as "young *Osric*," by Claudius. What is suggested despite Osric's flowery language is not polish, but a boor, a land rich country bumpkin trying to ape the manners of the court, not knowing when to remove his hat.[20]) The King's interruption allows Laertes to pass the point into his sleeve, as all politely look to Claudius. It makes the King's conclusion to his speech about the union in the cup, "And you the Judges bear a wary eye" (FF.5.2: 3740), pointing to the foils in the contenders' hands, a more "pointed" joke, for Claudius does not utter this, obviously, until the point is anointed, perhaps at the moment when he raises his cup to drink to Hamlet, and all eyes are upon the king.

The "**O, o, o, o**" of Hamlet's dying breath in the Folio, added after "The rest is silence" (*FF*.5.2: 3847), stressing his agony, his attempt to hold on to life, gives a graphic sense of his passing, not so neat as the Second Quarto, nor so ritualized. (And perhaps borrowed from the Quarto of *King Lear*, from which this very "O, o, o, o," as Lear's final exclamation was deleted.)

The last surprise is the alteration to Horatio's character in the Folio. The friend, so passive a shadow of the Prince throughout, emerges as the arbiter of the Danish throne. Horatio's lines, "I shall have **always** cause to speak, / And from his mouth / Whose voice will draw on more:" (*FF*.5.2: 3888–90), warns Fortinbras that the election to the Danish kingship can not come alone from the Norwegian's advantage (in marked contrast to the Second Quarto, where Horatio speaks a redundant resignation: "Of that I shall have **also** cause to speak, / And from his mouth, whose voice will draw **no** more" [*Q2.O2*: 5.2.380–81]).

Fortinbras must await the ratification of Hamlet's royal act in passing on to the Norwegian prince the succession. This is crucial to the sense of the play, that it end not in futility but in an orderly succession and that Hamlet has been able to act, not only in revenge, but also as a king, even if for a brief instant. It belies Fortinbras's words: "likely, had he been put on / To have prov'd most royally" (*FF*.5.2: 3897–98). It is the joint command of Horatio and Fortinbras at the end, Horatio representing "always" Hamlet's voice, like the joint command at the end of *King Lear* that leaves us with a sense of ambiguous resolution. In the Folio, Shakespeare is stressing that ambiguity. Horatio like Mark Antony in *Caesar* will deliver the funeral oration. It is he who now acts "royally." Seeming to be insignificant, the Folio substitutions portend much larger ones. Horatio will "always" or "continually" have "cause to speak," which implies Horatio's continued presence in the Danish court in a position of counsel. Hamlet's voice is not referred to as piteously past, but, on the contrary, in Horatio, its ratification will be "always" present to "draw on more." In the Folio, Hamlet has become his father and more than his father. The tongue-in-cheek success of Hamlet's last act is to become a ghost, whose "voice" the Danish throne promises to maintain.

6

Macbeth's Child

M_{ACBETH}, that bizarre play compounded of a tragedy of ambition and "a study in fear,"[1] works by reversal. If one accepts the chronology of literary historians that it can be dated after *Hamlet* and *Lear, Macbeth* reveals a further disillusionment in the playwright of these previous tragedies. Is it Shakespeare's ambition, then, that lies at the center of the drama, and equally, Shakespeare's fear? The method of the play, its mirror throwing up obverse images, makes deciphering difficult.

The world is set topsy turvy, "Eclipses in the Sun and Moon," or "Something . . . rotten" in the atmosphere of the state; that is familiar from the earlier dramas. *Macbeth* begins with the inhuman, however, the three witches. On the parapets of Elsinore the audience sees a ghost from the vantage of the men going around the ramparts. In *Macbeth* one is in the ring of the evil spirits themselves. Riddle, paradox, this has been part of the interrogatory mode of *Hamlet*, as Harry Levin describes its dominant rhetoric; *Lear* too has propounded—through its fool, the behavior of the King's daughters, Lear's violent rejection of his youngest—a set of questions. *Macbeth* starts with a riddle like a child's rhyme, set by a Satanic ring of women: "Fair is foul, and foul is fair. / Hover through the fog and filthy air."

That "fair" will be "foul" is easily understood as we watch all the promises made to Macbeth turn to curses. Banquo too will lose his life in grasping after the supernatural glimmer of the future that he unwisely demands, bluff fearlessness as foolish before the witches as Macbeth's silent "start" and stare. In *Macbeth* ghosts, apparitions, daggers, and spots of blood appear only to the guilty. Macbeth's single sight of Banquo's apparition at the banquet underscores this. The proof through Banquo, in retrospect, taints Banquo's sight of the witches—he too has been dreaming of the throne. What, however, of the "foul" that will be "fair"? Does it refer for the audience to the appearance of the witches, out of whose bearded, withered faces, fair prospects for the two heroes will shine? Is it the descent of James, king of Scotland and England, from the foul deeds of the play? Or does it propound a deeper riddle in the play. Yeats's line sings, "'Fair and foul are near of kin, / And fair needs foul,' I cried."[2] Does foul need fair? Is *Macbeth* a tragedy of love unrequited, where the tenderest passion is turned to anger? It is a paradox in *Macbeth* meant to catch our attention, repeated by the protagonist as he comes upon the stage, for the first time, act 1, scene 3: "So foul and fair a day I have not seen." That seems for a moment to answer it! Out of the foul deeds of treachery and bleak prospects of the battle has come the fair ending of success. Yet "fair," and "clear," the notion of spirits that "shine through" deeds will become images of hypocrisy. The very weather, the sound of birds chirping, turns ominous. Atmosphere in this play, even more than in *Hamlet,* makes drama, the lowering skies, day turned into night. (Its horror is often comic. Thus there is King Duncan commending the air of Macbeth's keep, "This castle hath a pleasant seat. The air / Nimbly and sweetly recommends itself. . . ." and Banquo seconding this "approval" with praise of the chirping "guest of summer, / The temple-haunting martlet . . ." [1.6.1–5]. The audience has just heard the exaggerated rhetoric of Lady Macbeth's, "The raven himself is hoarse / That croaks the fatal entrance of Duncan / Under my battlements." Duncan and Banquo pipe like flutes to the somber bass fiddle of Dracula's wife—the formula of chills and laughter.)

Shakespeare's riddle, hidden in such tricks of atmosphere, is not made plain until well into the play and then only by the aid of other riddles and continuous reversal, of fair for foul, foul for fair, on and on, things true by their opposites. "Are ye fantastical, or that indeed / Which outwardly ye show?" Banquo inquires of the witches. It is a question never answered and, (putting aside the interpolation of Hecate, Thomas Middleton's work) like the dagger and the ghost of Banquo, meant to be part of the world suspended between night and day, dream and waking, conscience and the uncanny. It is in this atmosphere of paradox, doubt, reality and fiction, belief and disbelief, that Shakespeare conceals his own question, paradox. It is upon sexual and religious fears not "fear" in general that the tragedy, *Macbeth,* plays.

The action begins with a child's riddle for what the play riddles is childlessness.[3] The witches come to tell Macbeth he will be king. Banquo unwisely interpolates his own claims. His general question speaks to a particular curiosity as Duncan's second great captain, dreams of kingship to which the witches are delighted to speak. "Why do you start and seem to fear / Things that do sound so fair?" Banquo asks Macbeth, before he addresses the witches. That repetition of "fair" alerts the ear to "foul." Macbeth is transfixed by the image of his own dreams, the bloody ambition to be king. He knows how foul that is, for he must have already thought of murder to achieve it. Banquo seems not to understand the witches, their faces, their words as literal representations of those faces, and is foolish enough to solicit promises for himself in Macbeth's presence. In drawing out their "fair" words, Banquo dooms his life. For Macbeth hears that he will not have children who will be kings when Banquo receives the promise; and the witches' gibe, "Not so happy, yet much happier" (1.3.71), rubs salt into this wound.

Macbeth's promise is tainted foul, doubly then, and Macbeth knows it, yet he can not speak of Banquo's taint upon it, will not speak of this particular threat to his wife Lady Macbeth: "Be innocent of the knowledge, dearest chuck, / Till thou applaud the deed" (3.2.50–51). Why would Macbeth deliberately keep his wife who seems so much fiercer, from knowledge of Banquo's promise and of the plot to murder Banquo?

The tragedy of the man, Macbeth, and the woman, Lady Macbeth, begins before the play. Something is wrong between them, something has happened, and it has to do with issue, children. Where are they? Why be ambitious to be king, if there is no succession to hand on?

A riddle reveals itself almost immediately in this regard as she urges her husband to the deed of murder.

> . . . . I have given suck, and know
> How tender 'tis to love the babe that milks me.
> I would, while it was smiling in my face,
> Have plucked my nipple from his boneless gums
> And dashed the brains out, had I so sworn as you
> Have done to this.
>
>   (1.7.60–65)

Has there been a pregnancy, a birth? The audience hears no more about it, and, in a play about the ambition to be king and to have one's seed inherit the kingship, this can not be an accident. We are faced with several possibilities. Has Lady Macbeth given her breast to a sister's child, someone else's? It seems unlikely, and equally unlikely that she has had a child by someone before Macbeth. Have they borne a child that has died—a boy? "His boneless gums," seems to confirm this, yet we have only one direct reference amid a host of suspicions.

It is a subject on which Macbeth remains silent. His silence is a measure of his character, deep dream life, anxiety, fears. His sense of slogging on through life despite the horror precedes even the first murders: "Come what come may, / Time and the hour runs through the roughest day" (1.3.164–65). The violence of his wife's lines, "while it was smiling in my face, / Have plucked my nipple from his boneless gums / And dashed the brains out," suggests King Lear's curse on his daughter's womb—anger at one's own flesh out of control. Is it anger from pain, a trauma that neither Macbeth or his lady can directly allude to it? Have the couple lost a child? Macbeth's "nothing is / But what is not" (1.3.155–56) refers overtly to the "thought" of "murder yet . . . but fantastical." May it not also refer to the death of a baby boy of "boneless gums" that still "shakes" his "single state of man"?

The mystery of this pair, Lady Macbeth and her lord, in pursuit of a throne for an heir who does not exist, their anger, ambition, mingled with compassion, point offstage to the playwright's pain, which Shakespeare felt but could not give voice to directly and therefore wound into his drama. A few lines after Lady Macbeth's cry that she would dash a baby to whom she felt tender love from her breast and knock its brains out in order to accomplish their ambition to be king and queen, Macbeth says in strange admiration;

Bring forth men-children only,
For thy undaunted mettle should compose
Nothing but males.

(1.7.81–83)

Why has the image of the baby murdered foully worked so on Macbeth that he surrenders his objections? "I dare do all that may become a man. / Who dares do more is none," he has told his wife just before her savage cry. The cruelest reading here is that Macbeth is impotent to produce any babies. This would explain the play's obsession with being a "man," acting as a "man," which Macbeth turns on the murderers of Banquo. Has Lady Macbeth *hallucinated* a baby at her breasts?

The image forces Macbeth's mind back to the deed that has so repelled him, but not only because it is an accusation of impotence. The reference to a baby for which Lady Macbeth has felt love brought to a sudden violent death calls on a common grief. It shakes Macbeth's manhood because it speaks to his tenderness, the pain of a dead child. This is part of the irrational doubling of the play, the man of conscience, shadowed constantly by conscience, who nevertheless becomes a grimmer and grimmer murdered—the seeker whose belief betrays him to despair. It is Macbeth's tenderness toward his lady that steels him to be brutal to a king who has been like a father, but it is the image of the child dashed from her breasts, his own fatherhood betrayed, that betrays him to that tenderness. Macbeth sees his wife speaking as a man and commiserates with her in the crazed grief that the language expresses by wishing her the mother of males. It would explain her fierceness by reversal, for, being deprived of "How tender 'tis to love," she has gone to the opposite, cursing her own breasts:

> . . . . Come to my woman's breasts
> And take my milk for gall, you murd'ring ministers,
> Wherever in your sightless substances
> You wait on nature's mischief!
>
> (1.5.51–54)

"Nature's mischief" is an apt term for a crib death, a sudden illness in childhood, and for the death of children, which will be emphasized in act 4, scenes 2 and 3. The language and action are so cruel as to cause some critics to question Shakespeare's taste and, therefore, authorship of the lines, but they throw into harsh light, the brutality that Macbeth assumes, even as his lady breaks down. The shouts with which the children of Macduff are murdered as Macbeth's madness reaches its zenith: "What you egg! / Young fry of treachery!" (4.2.91–92) are metaphors of the ditch world.[4] The images speak back to the ditch, "Ditch-delivered," to conception, breeding, the world of the witches' cauldron. How to explain the death of children except as "nature's mischief"? It will give Macduff's arm almost supernatural power.[5] Cheated of an heir by crib death, such revengeful anger no less would steel Macbeth and his wife to their ambition, cheated before they begin their plots. They have no child that we know of, only hopes, and a riddling allusion to a baby at Lady Macbeth's breasts, dashed in a metaphor to death. Scorning her husband's tenderness, Lady Macbeth uses a concealed simile of Macbeth as a woman with a breast: "Yet do I fear thy nature. / It is too full o' the milk of human kindness" (1.5.15–16). This sense of pathos and of nature turned against itself runs through the play. The audience looks backward to the fatal look forward with which the witches tease Macbeth and Banquo. The murder of Macduff's children is anticipated in the rightful fears of Duncan's sons and the attempt on Fleance, Banquo's boy. Macduff's cries hearing the news of his family's murder may echo the stifled cry of Macbeth. For when Malcolm attempts to quiet Macduff, the latter's outrage speaks to the play's root:

> Be comforted.
> Let's make us med'cines of our great revenge
> To cure this deadly grief.

[To which Macduff shouts] "He has no children."

(4.3.250–53)

The audience knows that Malcolm's seed will not inherit the throne. Malcolm, no matter how blameless and innocent of the charges he brings against himself, is tainted as patriarch by impotence. Malcolm acts only through the deeds of mighty captains, like his father, Duncan, before him. One is reminded of the beginning of *Macbeth* when Malcolm thanks the sergeant "Who like a good and hardy soldier fought / 'Gainst my captivity" (1.2.5–6). Others have to rescue Malcolm, assert the rights of his dynasty, seed, not his own arm. Macduff's disparagement then bites in a double sense; Malcolm can not feel or pass on an inheritance. Malcolm's previous assertion of sexual appetite is almost too broadly comic.

The audience hears again the witches' riddle. A man without children, Macbeth, wishes not only to be king but to reign through his children after death. In trying to murder his competitor, Banquo, and the latter's boy, Fleance, Macbeth reaches toward the future to ensure a phantom succession. It is the obsession of a man who lives a tortured dream life. Are ambitious hopes and frustrations what one might expect of a playwright who had lost a son, Hamnet, dreamed of his daughters, and now found himself wondering what would come after him?

Women, witches, come to propound the riddle to Macbeth appropriate in the context of this male and female die set spinning by the conflict. Crossing the paradox of childlessness is the anxiety of male and female identity. Shakespeare had children surviving after his only son, Hamnet's death, but they were women. His hopes for a son frustrated, his wife perhaps past childbearing, his fantasy in a reversal of roles acts itself out in the play. There are other powerful women in Shakespeare, Portia, for instance, and the growing realistic conventions of the stage must have made their portrayal by men a provocation to liberation no less than the example of Queen Elizabeth. Here were ideal mates—smart, capable, yet filled with an aura of sexual romance. They still work magic upon the minds of the audience. In a sense, Lady Macduff is one of these, despite the pathos that overwhelms her end: sharp-tongued, decisive in her judgment, and with an edge of humor in her speech. In studied contrast to Portia, however, Lady Macduff refuses to exchange roles, male for female. She dies, a martyr to the notion of women as an ideal whose existence should be beyond the brutality of ambition and revenge.

> Whither should I fly?
> I have done no harm. But I do remember now
> I am in this earthly world, where to do harm
> Is often laudable, to do good sometime
> Accounted dangerous folly. Why then, alas,
> Do I put up that womanly defense
> To say I have done no harm?
>
> (4.2.79–85)

Shakespeare has set this ideal as a foil to Lady Macbeth, who is in revolt against her role as a woman. The latter, in a soliloquy that is a stage ritual of metamorphosis, of transformation from the idea of female pity into male bestiality, tries to assimilate in the place of sexual heat, a lust for power. One can see the three witches as Macbeth's nightmare of his wife. Lady Macbeth sanitizes the witches, their role in her reference to them, as "fate and metaphysical aid" (1.5.29). Lady Macbeth's speeches parody the crones as she tries to assume power over the world of beasts, take them for her familiars as the witches take cats, toads. What else is heard in that speech?

> The raven himself is hoarse
> The croaks the fatal entrance of Duncan
> Under my battlements. Come, you spirits
> That tend on mortal thoughts, unsex me here,
> And fill me, from the crown to the toe, top-full
> Of direst cruelty!
>
> (1.5.42–47)

This is a direct invitation to possession by the spirits of evil, a ritual of witchcraft. Yet what is asked for, more than just power, is transformation into evil—equated with passage into a principle of male action. Milk from the female breast seen as pity is felt as despicable, likewise the breast, because it leaks pity. Lady Macbeth alludes to this: "Yet do I fear thy nature. / It is too full o' the milk of human kindness." The will to transgress against nature, one's own nature, is an obsession of the play.

> . . . Make thick my blood;
> Stop up the access and passage to remorse,
> That no compunctious visitings of nature
> Shake my fell purpose nor keep peace between
> The effect and it!
>
> (1.5.47–51)

The rhetoric rises toward hysteria. Macbeth's final line "Hold, enough!" in act 5 (that despairing tongue-in-cheek shout of damnation) is heard here as his lady offers herself to the creatures of the night.

> . . . . Come to my woman's breasts
> And take my milk for gall, you murd'ring ministers,
> Wherever in your sightless substances
> You wait on nature's mischief! Come, thick night,
> And pall thee in the dunnest smoke of hell,
> That my keen knife see not the wound it makes,
> Nor heaven peep through the blanket of the dark
> To cry "Hold, hold!"
>
> (1.5.51–58)

Lady Macbeth wishes to be something beyond a witch, to exchange female for male. Her overstress, since finally she will collapse back, pathetic, broken, signals a wound to her womanhood. Like the act of ambition, it has happened antecedent to the play. We feel its effect, but can never riddle out its cause. Banquo asks of the witches.

> . . . You should be women,
> And yet your beards forbid me to interpret
> That you are so.
>
> (1.3.46–48)

This is the condition of Lady Macbeth,[6] and it recalls King Lear questioning the female nature of his daughters. While Lady Macbeth will not appear literally bearded, her attempt to take on a

male character and the ambiguity of her sexual nature betrays her
to madness at the end.

There is confusion of male and female from the first moment of
the play, for we have seen these witches and wondered on their
sex with Banquo. What is the nature of man—Macbeth tries to
define it honorably, but his wife will have none of that. Lady Macbeth's stress on its meaning as power, a man, male, as a principle
of pitiless ambition, her Elizabethan machismo, makes her repression of Macbeth's sexual role and her own, the absence of heirs (or
"hairs" as Northumberland grimly jokes) loom more obvious. The
word "beast" in this context has an obscene but paradoxical echo.

> *Macb.* I dare do all that may become a man.
> Who dares do more is none.
> *Lady.* What beast was't then
> That made you break this enterprise to me?
> When you durst do it, then you were a man;
> And to be more than what you were, you would
> Be so much more the man.
>
> (1.7.51–57)

Macbeth will responds to this, finally, with a bizarre admiration,
one that for the first time speaks of his hopes of an heir, of seed,
copulation, and returns Lady Macbeth, obliquely, to her female
role.

> Bring forth men-children only,
> For thy undaunted mettle should compose
> Nothing but males.
>
> (1.7.81–83)

The response is evoked, however, not by the direct reproach of
his manhood, but by a speech in which Lady Macbeth has spoken
of her maternal tenderness, the pleasure of a baby sucking at her
breasts, only to rage that she is willing to knock its brains out to
fulfill her ambition. Again she seems to be cursing her female
parts, despising them, and the audience is left with an image of
anguish, self-horror. Her images imply that her partner is a coward, less of a male than she is willing to be. Macbeth by implication
is womanly, pity filled. In assuming this identity, Lady Macbeth
shames her husband, and he does become the stereotype of a passive woman, assenting to be led in opposition to what he knows is
a better definition of a man. The passage ends fittingly with the
language of reversal, fair is foul: "Away, and mock the time with

fairest show; / False face must hide what the false heart doth know" (1.7.92–93).

Are you a man? Lady Macbeth cries over and over to her husband. This will echo King Lear's "thou hast power to shake my manhood thus" (*FF.* 1.4: 815). Men in front of these determined women begin to break apart, or threaten to do so. Yet Lear's oldest daughter, Gonerill, will kill herself, after poisoning the younger, Regan, taking the route of Ophelia. Gertrude too commits a kind of suicide taking up the poisoned chalice as if knowing, choosing like Ophelia to chastise by example, while the men, stoically, even with some humor, endure their fate.

The apostrophe to manhood is sounded in the instructions to the murderers of Banquo by Macbeth in which he echoes his wife's rhetoric. Is it a parody? He knows that going beyond certain limits is a disgrace to manhood. Macbeth's sneering Christian reference, "gospeled," is in despite of the "Merciful powers" to whom Banquo prayed for protection against evil thoughts.

> *Macb.* . . . Are you so gospeled
> To pray for this good man and for his issue,
> Whose heavy hand hath bowed you to the grave
> And beggared yours for ever?
> 1. *Mur.* We are men, my liege.
> *Macb.* Ay, in the catalogue ye go for men,
> As hounds and greyhounds, mongrels, spaniels, curs,
> Shoughs, water-rugs, and demi-wolves are clept
> All by the name of dogs. The valued file
> Distinguishes the swift, the slow, the subtle,
> The housekeeper, the hunter, every one
> According to the gift which bounteous nature
> Hath in him closed; whereby he does receive
> Particular addition, from the bill
> That writes them all alike; and so of men.
> Now, if you have a station in the file,
> Not i' the worst rank of manhood, say't;

(3.1.95–111)

Lady Macbeth cries to her husband, starting at Banquo's ghost: "What, quite unmanned in folly?" (3.4.90). And again, Macbeth asserts his manhood:

> What man dare, I dare.
> Approach thou like the rugged Russian bear,
> The armed rhinoceros, or the Hyrcan tiger;
> Take any shape but that, and my firm nerves

Shall never tremble. Or be alive again
And dare me to the desert with thy sword.
If trembling I inhabit then, protest me
The baby of a girl. Hence, horrible shadow!
Unreal mock'ry, hence!

(3.4.122–30)

That final fillip, "protest me / The baby of a girl," is an image that degrades, mocks the notion of female courage, but, in its wording, it seems to allude to Macbeth's fear of no heirs, his contempt and fear of the child. It is no accident then that in the charade it is a child who appears twice, that "unreal mock'ry" which dogs him throughout (4.1.87–120).

* * *

At the end, like a baited dog or bear tied to the stake, Macbeth will endure the thrusts of fate with the stubborn tenacity of an animal—even though a fear crazed one. In doing so consciously, Macbeth will win for himself some sympathy from the audience that feels as it does in front of Lear (not Edgar, who is being described) on the heath, a man stripped and howling, the dread of their own nakedness, "the thing it self: unaccomo- / dated man . . . a poor, bare, forked A- /nimal" (FF.3.4:1886–88).

In *King Lear*, the copulating world of nature has roared about the King's ears: "The Wren goes too't, and the small gilded Fly / Does lecher in my sight. . . . Too't Luxury pell-mell. . . . The Fitchew, nor / the soiled Horse goes too't with a more riotous appe- / tite." (FF.4.6: 2558–59, 2562, and 2565–67). Hamlet's excursion to the country has been to sit and philosophize in a graveyard, drowning or interment it seems is the only escape from the castle. Yet the line between the kingdom of evil and good, darkness and light, human and animal, is still sharply drawn. Hamlet puts on his insanity as Edgar puts on Poor Tom—though the role threatens the actor. In Macbeth and his lady, this line is dissolved. Lady Macbeth will not become a witch, nor her master a warlock, but they will be "mocked" by a "horrible shadow" world. Imaginary daggers, spots of blood, and the ghost of a murdered man in the interior of the castle will be abetted by a landscape of half human animals without.[7] The sense of a foul ditch nature that has run like a current through *Lear* and *Hamlet* is here given its full current and not the natural, but the unnatural, poisonous. In the language of the witches, a tide of filth rises from the bog and fen of the British Islands through the heavy drops of vapor, in a cauldron of fog, marsh: "Toad, that under cold stone / Days and nights has thirty-one / Swelt'red venom sleeping got, . . . Fillet of a fenny snake, . . . Eye of newt, and toe of frog, / Wool of bat, and tongue of dog, / Adder's fork, and blindworm's sting, / Lizard's leg, and howlet's wing; . . ." And to this scurf of horror all sorts of exotica is pinched in: "Witch's mummy, maw and gulf / Of the ravined salt-sea shark, / Root of hemlock, digged i' the dark, / Liver of blaspheming Jew, / Gall of goat, and slips of yew / Slivered in the moon's eclipse; / Nose of Turk and Tartar's lips. . . ." Its apotheosis is in the exultant cry of Lady Macbeth, who gives her sexual parts over to evil, the devil, but they meet in the world of the ditch, the abortions and miscarriages of the poor in damp ends of country lanes: "Finger of birth-strangled babe / Ditch-delivered by a drab: / Make the gruel thick and slab . . ." (4.1.5–33).

The offstage voice is heard in this last image, suggesting a dead child, an infant mourned in the twisted liturgy of the witches echoing the nightmares of Lady Macbeth. In that howling there is some awful, inhuman pain. It is man, woman regressing into an animal shape, and, in a premonition of Darwin, the witches finish the cauldron's ingredients, crying, "Cool it with a baboon's blood, / Then the charm is firm and good" (4.1.37–38).

Macbeth's charges to the witches sound remarkably like Lear's directions to the awful powers of the storm across the heath: "Crack Nature['] s molds, all germains spill at once / That makes ungrateful Man . . . " (F.F.3.2: 1663–64). Like Lear's speech, Macbeth's is an invocation to the wind, the ancient storm gods that though plural, have an uncanny relationship to the Hebrew Spirit that has brought the world from chaos and can return to it *"tohu vebohoo,* chaos and confusion," or "without form or life."[8] Like his wife, Lady Macbeth, at the height of her self delusion, a dark wizard, the king of Scotland incants " . . . though the treasure / Of nature's germens tumble all together, / Even till destruction sicken—answer me" (4.1.60–62). Yet Macbeth's speech is subtly different from Lear's. It is not the breaking of molds, but "the seeds of everything yet uncreated," to quote the Folger Library edition's explanation, being shaken into a madness that brings on the storm flattening the corn, trees, blowing down churches, toppling "castles . . . palaces and pyramids . . . Even till destruction sicken." It is not the destruction of the seed as in *Lear,* but its confusion, that suggests itself to Macbeth in his agony. Desperation to have an heir and being heirless, without root in the world, is tormenting Macbeth. All his murder is for naught he cries, only to put a crown on Banquo's children's head. Claudius in *Hamlet* might complain on the same theme—but he doesn't. The thought never troubles his head because Shakespeare is not interested in assuming his persona.

It is Hamlet who sees that, as a nephew, he is so close as to almost be engendered of Claudius, the latter assuming an even closer place, a father's, in marrying the Prince's mother. In the grip of the incestuous family relations, Hamlet calls ironically to his villainous uncle as the Prince is forced to leave for England, "Mother." It is an endless joke of the family murders, the blood ties. Hamlet will curse copulation, order his bride to a nunnery, and so betray the seed of the royal family, his own seed, dooming its succession. Lear too will curse his own progeny, one by one, and, at the end, curses fulfilled, die bereft of all heirs. Yet these concerns are never allowed to dominate the tragedies of *Hamlet* and *Lear*. It is only in *Macbeth* that the horror of childlessness is given full rein by the playwright.

It explains, perhaps, the resort to the supernatural, the ditch world of nature. Frustrated of the mysteries of birth, Macbeth and his wife turn to a world of animism, invoke rooks, owls, witches, hoping to make a pact with the night. Lady Macbeth hears the raven croaking itself hoarse as Duncan rides under her castle walls, an owl shrieking, the cry of crickets as the king is being killed (2.2.5). At the point of murdering Banquo, Macbeth with tenderness turns to his lady and calls her "dearest chuck," deriving erotic tenderness it would seem from the deaths he is plotting. Is horror a substitution for Macbeth's doubtful life in bed?

Can one avoid the implication of sexual impotence? What is all the discussion of manhood between the Thane and his lady tending to but that? Far off in the play, we will hear Malcolm's claim to boundless lechery as a mocking echo of Macbeth's inability to perform.

> . . . But there's no bottom, none,
> In my voluptuousness. Your wives, your daughters,
> Your matrons, and your maids could not fill up
> The cistern of my lust; and my desire
> All continent impediments would o'erbear
> That did oppose my will.
>
> (4.3.69–74)

Macbeth decides he can not murder, but, at the gibe of Lady Macbeth that he is no man, changes his mind (also after an image of the child dashed from her breast, their common loss): "Art thou afeared / To be the same in thine own act and valor / As thou art in desire?" (1.7.43–45). Husband and wife do not speak of their sexual frustration directly; how can they? Like the dead child, the passionless bed is far too painful. Their unhappy bed may be the consequence of the loss of the child. Yet it gives both such tenderness for each other that the audience, which senses a pain never articulated except by indirection, is drawn despite morality to sympathy.

Does the act of murder rob Macbeth and his wife of the very kingdom they desire, sex, which lies in the bosom of sleep, dreams? Lady Macbeth disparages sleep when she urges her husband on: "swinish sleep," she calls the drunken slumber of Duncan. The Thane of Glamis and Cawdor cries that he has murdered sleep. It is no simile; it is fact. When the dagger appears before him, he becomes aware of the hold that dream has on him and the threat it is to his own nature. Sleep and death are in correspondence: "Now o'er the one half-world / Nature seems dead, and wicked dreams abuse / The curtained sleep. Witchcraft celebrates . . ." (2.1.58–60). Lady Macbeth will equate the sleeping and the dead, bidding Macbeth be bold, and go in herself to smear the daggers of the grooms with blood ("The sleeping and the dead / Are but as pictures" [2.2.70–71]) and will refer his fear to "the eye of childhood." Her punishment will be terrible for it is the blood that she smears upon the sleeping from the dead that will pursue her to self-destruction.

Still, why should the voice cry out to Macbeth, "Sleep no more! / Macbeth does murder sleep," and provoke from the Thane a piteous praise for what he has lost forever? "Balm of hurt minds"; what hurt? Does the restless torment to which sleep has been balm lie before the murder, in the act of ambition? Alfred Harbage points this out: "At some unknown time for some unknown reason Macbeth has corrupted in pride, and has contemplated the sale of his soul as certainly as Faustus."[9] This points, however, to the other "unknown time," the dead child's, and the couple's present impotence.

Why are there so many rooks, owls, birds, clamoring at Macbeth and his Lady throughout the tragedy. (I remember a sleepless night in the country, lying awake in the morning, hearing the cry of the birds on and on.) The clucks of other birds as well haunt Lennox's line about the owl on the eve and morning of Duncan's murder: "The obscure bird / Clamored the livelong night" (2.3.61–62).

Unable to sleep, unable to perform, the hero is prey to the voices not of dying, but, worse, of light being born, light and birth of which he will be cheated. It is the time when the Ghost in *Hamlet* walks before Horatio and the guards; yet, in the latter play, it is more stage effect than metaphysical image. The opening of *Macbeth* is set just before the world sinks into darkness ("ere the set of sun"), but the play goes in murky light. The ghosts, the murderers, walk between midnight and the dawn.[10] The cry of the "obscure bird," like the clamor of the drunken porter, speaks to impotence, the nightmare of Macbeth given comic utterance in the clown's soliloquy—like the Fool of *Lear*, privileged to speak the truth to the world. The knocking at Heaven's gate is real knocking, the gibing at sexual impotence in drunkenness mocks the impotence of those reeling in murder.

The birds of *Macbeth* are nested in Macduff's castle as well. As in Banquo's "temple-haunting martlet," there is a rejoinder to the ravens and owls of the Macbeths. Yet there is something unnatural about Macduff too. If Macbeth is the owl, "The obscure bird," then the allusion is direct. Lady Macduff says of her husband, "He wants the natural touch. For the poor wren, / (The most diminutive of birds) will fight, / Her young ones in her nest, against the owl" (4.2.11–13). In Lady Macduff's banter with her son, this language points to the fable in the play, the coming horror, which is bestial. (We recall Lady Macbeth's reproach to her husband: "What beast was't then / That made you break this enterprise to me?" [1.7.53–54]—a beast that is unnatural, a horror of the ditch, where the dead Banquo lies, a breeding place of worms and flies.)

Wife. [Lady Macduff]. . . . How will you live?
Son. As birds do, mother.
Wife. What, with worms and flies?
Son. With what I get, I mean; and so do they.
Wife. Poor bird! thou'dst never fear the net nor lime,
The pitfall nor the gin.

(4.2.35–40)

The murderer, stabbing the prim boy, shouts, as if he were the spawn of birds, or frogs in the ditch: "What, you egg! / [stabbing him] / Young fry of treachery!" (4.2.91–93).

There is a peculiar crossing in this play of the backdrop of the natural British world so particular and present on the heath of *King Lear*, the graveyard in *Hamlet*, and the interior world of the playhouse, the doomed castles, Elsinore, Macbeth's, Macduff's, Forres, Dunsinane. The effect of these two worlds shifting at once through the consciousness of Macbeth is to create a vertigo in which he loses all sense of reality. Among the exotica of the witches' ingredients are the barnyard mysteries of horror. The natural world is gone awry though through Macbeth's impotence, aborted or thwarted. He has botched his manhood. It is a sexual barnyard in which the witches stir. The porter's speech goes from Hell's gate to inability to procreate. Reeling drunk, in liquor or blood, one can not, as the porter says, "stand to," perform, muster an erection. At the moment of murder, comedy jokes with the underriding fear of Macbeth and his Lady.

This anxiety is summed up in those bleak lines when, having come to kingship, Macbeth finds its power has no taste. The images "fruitless," "barren," stress sexual emptiness in his world, not just lack of seed.

> Upon my head they placed a fruitless crown
> And put a barren scepter in my gripe,
> Thence to be wrenched with an unlineal hand,
> No son of mine succeeding.

> (3.1.65–68)

If Macbeth had children his conflict with Banquo might be seen differently, but it is only a theoretical line of succession Macbeth murders for. He is in the grip of the powers of the night, and in that kingdom he is barren and fruitless, the admission of which is too frightening. Crazed with anger at the sight of so many heirs of Banquo's as against his fruitless marriage, Macbeth decides to murder the children and wife of Macduff, misreading the witches' warning against the latter. The murder of those innocents, particularly the young boy, is a chilling reminder of Macbeth's vacant loins. He has shielded Lady Macbeth from the knowledge of his murder of Banquo, fearing her reservations, an echo of which we hear. Again, her breakdown occurs immediately after the murder of the Macduff family—linking it in the line of action, although it is never directly commented on. The babies Lady Macbeth so glibly boasted she would have "dashed the brains out" have now been sacrificed, and it seems to be the act that has unhinged her. She mumbles to herself, "The Thane of Fife had a wife. Where is she / now?" like a child's rhyme (5.1.38–39). Lady Macbeth is innocent of these murders, and yet, since she has provoked the chain of action with her vaunt, not innocent at all. She is drowned now in her own milk, in terror, finding herself without feeling except of dread. The echo of the witches cackle is clear.

Pour in sow's blood that hath eaten
Her nine farrow;

(4.1.71–72)

Lady Macbeth has eaten up her own brood. Her words have de-
voured the children she might have had.

Pig, toad, cat, bear, wild horses: the forest howls at the two Macbeths, moves, shifts, shakes in storm. The tempest in *Lear* rises,
then falls, but it has no end in *Macbeth*. The Thane and his wife
have imagined that they can take on the character of the rooks of
their castle, the owls, their language presumes it. "The obscure
bird" of night, which hints at the obscuring of the crime, is but
illusion. Unable to sleep both husband and wife loose their footing
in the real world. They have not merely murdered Duncan, their
king, they have "murdered sleep," as Macbeth himself calls out.

"Sleep no more!" a voice sounds in Macbeth's head. It is not
merely conscience, or rather conscience in this case has to do with
the murder of a father. Macbeth has dreamed of being Duncan's
heir, son. The murder is set in motion at the moment when he is
frustrated of that by Malcolm's nomination to Cumberland. Lady
MacBeth has recognized in Duncan's face her father's. This patrici-
dal terror is part of theme of the dramas that have preceded them.
The ambivalence of children and fathers, the nightmare of no
heirs, the fear of no succession, is, in *Macbeth*, directly linked to its
protagonists' impotence. The couple, hounded by sleeplessness,
driven to violent despair in their bed, become the actors in their
waking nightmare.

By the conclusion of *Macbeth*, the obsessions that make up the
play's nightmare—patricide, childlessness, sexual desire without
satisfaction, the image of the world as meaningless, as chaos—
appeared, even to the playwright, as bordering on voluptuous in-
dulgence. A minor character, Ross, one of Macbeth's defecting captains, observes, ". . . violent sorrow seems / A modern ecstasy."
The word "ecstasy," which in other Shakespearian usage implies
love's rapture, almost erotic bliss,[11] recalls Macbeth's strange use of
it in referring to the anxiety in which he has lived after murdering
King Duncan.

. . . Better be with the dead,
Whom we, to gain our peace, have sent to peace,
Than on the torture of the mind to lie
In restless ecstasy.

(3.2.21–24)

This suggests a sexual gratification or powerful stimulus in the horror, the restlessness, the sorrow. So when Ross, coming to inform Macduff of the loss of the latter's wife and children, uses this word, it is a self-accusing, almost sarcastic, reference. The country, Scotland, has been violated, as the context of Ross's words make clear. All the captains must share responsibility.

> Alas, poor country,
> Almost afraid to know itself! It cannot
> Be called our mother, but our grave; where nothing,
> But who knows nothing, is once seen to smile;
> Where signs and groans, and shrieks that rent the air,
> Are made, not marked; where violent sorrow seems
> A modern ecstasy.

(4.3.185–91)

A sense of sexual violation echoes as well in Malcolm's unexpected feint to uncover Macduff's intentions, in which the legitimate heir to Duncan's throne pretends to an unprincipled sexual appetite. Malcolm's impotence links him to Macbeth, who has usurped his throne—both of them we, the audience, know, will be cheated of succession. Both of them are, somehow, less than men. The notion of the country no longer a mother calls us back to Lady Macbeth's cruel soliloquy giving up her motherhood. The final child's riddle, which concludes the play and brings Macbeth to doom, smacks of this mockery of maleness through motherhood. "What's he / That was not born of woman?" Macbeth asks. Can one truly avoid being born of woman? Does not the riddle tease the notion of a manhood untainted by pity, here equated with womanliness?

The theme is revolved in the conversation between Malcolm and Macduff, when the murder of the latter's children is announced and the gruff captain bursts into exclamations of fury and surprise.

> *Macd.* . . . O hell-kite! All?
> What, all my pretty chickens and their dam
> At one fell swoop?
> *Mal.* Dispute it like a man.
> *Macd.* I shall do so;
> But I must also feel it as a man. . . .
> O, I could play the woman with mine eyes
> And braggart with my tongue! But, gentle heavens,
> Cut short all intermission. Front to front. . . .
> *Mal.* This tune goes manly.

(4.3.254–59, 268–70 and 274)

The death of Macbeth plays upon this same theme of manhood, while returning us to the violence of a birth that threatens tragedy. There is something more to the riddle of the witches than meets the eye. Is it a mere trick of coincidence that Macduff's birth has been premature, so that the prophecy that "none of woman born / Shall harm Macbeth" (4.1.90–91) may be fulfilled? Or does Macbeth's reply to Macduff's vaunt, "Despair thy charm! / And let the angel whom thou still hast served / Tell thee, Macduff was from his mother's womb / Untimely ripped" (5.8.17–20) play on what has haunted the manhood of the doomed king of Scotland. Why should the language of manhood and child death, which spoke at the fatal monent when Lady Macbeth steeled her husband to an act against his will, now call from him lines that speak again about the surrender of manliness?

> Accursed be that tongue that tells me so,
> For it hath cowed my better part of man!
>
> (5.8.21–22)

Does Macduff's claim to be a child snatched from crib death flash before Macbeth the memory of his own baby son's death, with boneless gums? Does this, rather than the "juggling" of the witches, which he might have suspected, unnerve him? Macduff has spoken Macbeth's secret, touched the latter's unspoken riddle.

The playwright can not adjure the temptation of a final sermon on the theme of fatherhood, engendering, sons. In a last bit of pathos at the end we see the gruff warrior, Siward, lose his son and bear the loss, "manly." With a bitter irony, Shakespeare allows the staunch, but rather cold, father a pun, "hairs, heirs," in his brave farewell.

> Had I as many sons as I have hairs,
> I would not wish them to a fairer death.
> And so his knell is knolled.
> *Mal.* He's worth more sorrow,
> And that I'll spend for him.
> *Siw.* He's worth no more.
> They say he parted well and paid his score,
> And so, God be with him!

This is something too dispassionate for the loss of a son and heir. It speaks not only to Macbeth's exaggerated grief, it also speaks to Shakespeare's and is the far off knell (I believe) for his dead son, Hamnet. Only at the end of his career, in *The Tempest,* will the ghosts of succession return, and in a pastoral, go round about his head.

* * *

To leave *Macbeth* wholly on a personal note is a disservice to the riddle. Whatever secrets of Shakespeare's life lie at its center, as with its companion tragedies, *Hamlet* and *King Lear,* what strikes the audience and the reader is the breadth of theological protest against the world as perceived. The latest of the three, *Macbeth* is the bleakest. The audience is following the reflections of a character not unlike Claudius in *Hamlet,* as if the latter were to rise up from the altar, dragging his fruitless knocking at the gates of Heaven about his heels as he stumbles on through not one, not two, but many murders. Macbeth is not a poisoner, but a hero, a captain of reckless bravery. His anguish against the tragedy of his ambition, his inability to shake the shadow world, begins to sound a protest against human life, its conditions, that goes beyond the boundaries of *Hamlet* and *King Lear. Lear* has looked backward in remorse, to a world of homeless wretches he might have helped: "O I have ta['] ne / Too little care of this" (*FF.*3.4: 1813–14). He rages at rain, wind, thunder, and fire, "Servile Ministers" (*FF.* 3.2: 1676) that look on at his pain. Whether Lear believes or does not believe in Heaven is in doubt. Macbeth like Hamlet believes, but Macbeth's torment devils him, bends back belief to disbelief. Macbeth begins by juggling with theological reflection.

> . . . If the assassination
> Could trammel up the consequence, and catch,
> With his surcease, success, that but this blow
> Might be the be-all and the end-all here,
> But here, upon this bank and shoal of time,
> We'ld jump the life to come.
>
> (1.7.2–7)

In this context scholars believe "jump" means "risk," but to "jump the life to come" is absurd if one believes. Macbeth, however, will "jump" despite belief at Lady Macbeth's insistence. The verb "jump" seems to retain a sense of its meaning "to spring" for Macbeth's "risk" is also a leap beyond into an abyss. (Kenneth Muir suggests that "jump" may mean "evade," though at the end of the soliloquy with "heaven's cherubin," trumpeting the bloody deed, evasion appears to Macbeth impossible.)[12] Thoughts of tumbling but landing in a worse position "haunt" him. Even in the present, the "here" in which the risk must be taken—"here, upon this bank and shoal of time"—Macbeth turns back for a moment from the leap. He realizes that the act of killing a king will be "Bloody instructions, which, being taught, return / To plague the inventor." This is very different from Hamlet trying to discern whether the devil is intent, through the Ghost, on tricking the Prince into an act of self-damnation. Implicit in Macbeth's lines "But in these cases / We still have judgment here . . ." is the knowledge of judgment *there*, in the world to come. Macbeth knows that pursuing his ambition must cheat him of the future world. It is only for this future world in which his heirs will reign that Macbeth follows his ambition. He juggles, sees its futility, turns back only to "jump" later.

The very act of ambition for Macbeth, therefore, is one of despair, since he is aware that it condemns him to "deep damnation." He sees "heaven's cherubin, horsed / Upon the sightless couriers of the air," with their trumpets blowing the "horrid deed in every eye, / That tears shall drown the wind" (1.7.20–25). The mixed metaphor of the mote troubling the mind's eye, the ear, hearing, expresses the violence of his self-repugnance, "self-abuse" as Lady Macbeth later hears Macbeth call his malady.

Why embark on such a mad course? Macbeth knows that the witches are creatures of evil, "instruments of darkness" as Banquo cautions, counseling passivity. Macbeth's balancing of alternatives seems specious, and he is aware that the fair promise is followed in his imagination by the fantasy of murder.

> This supernatural soliciting
> Cannot be ill; cannot be good. If ill,
> Why hath it given me earnest of success,
> Commencing in a truth? I am Thane of Cawdor.
> If good, why do I yield to that suggestion
> Whose horrid image does unfix my hair
> And make my seated heart knock at my ribs
> Against the use of nature?
>
> (1.3.144–51)

The paradox, difficult to understand unless we hear the political echoes of countries in which America is "the great devil," may be precisely that Macbeth is caught in a theological crisis that makes his choice inevitable. Religious language characterizes his speech from the beginning. In act 1, scene 7, he debates the question of judgment in a future life and paints a picture of a heaven swarming with angels and babes soliciting pity. In the second scene of act 2, he breaks down, describing how the servants of Duncan said their prayers and trying to whisper "Amen," the word stuck in the Thane's throat. There is malicious laughter in the way Macbeth taunts the murders to their deed with the voice of a preacher— "Are you so gospeled / To pray for this good man and for his issue" (3.1.95–96) and "Your spirits shine through you" (3.1.142)—so it is not a surprise to find among his invocation of curses and powers, "untie the winds, and let them fight / Against the churches" (4.1.54–55); and again, as the line of kings from Banquo lengthens: "What, will the line stretch out to the crack of doom?" (4.1.131). (It is Macbeth's pale opposite, Malcolm, whose lines also echo with religions allusion: "Angels are bright still, though the brightest fell. / Though all things foul would wear the brows of grace, / Yet grace must still look so" (4.3.25–27].[13]) In a crisis of faith, the king of Scotland needs the devil to confirm his belief in something. In this sense, Macbeth is indeed a tragic hero, because he is struggling with the theological dilemma of his century. Unable to summon angels, the Thane is open to the suggestion of witches. Basil Willey details just such a struggle in his book, *The Seventeenth Century Background.*

> During the greater part of the century Satan remained the most living figure in the current mythology. "God" had been rationalized through centuries of theology, and was now receding still further into the inconceivable as the frontiers of natural causation were pushed back and back. But Satan, symbol of how much! of the endless indignation of the subconscious against the mind-forged manacles, of fear, and pride, and rebelliousness—Satan was still far more than an allegory which could be explained in conceptual language. . . . When "God" becomes a scientific hypothesis, almost identifiable with absolute space, it is not surprising that the religious consciousness should express itself through "Satan." It is probably for this reason that those who, as the scientific philosophy strengthened its hold, adhered tenaciously to a supernatural world-view, felt that they must cling to Satan in order to keep God. The idea that to abandon belief in witches was to begin on the slippery slope to atheism was a common one at this time. . . . Browne's views on witchcraft are well known, and may be best read in the *Religio Medici;*
>
>> For my part I have ever believed, and do now know, that there are Witches: they that doubt of these, do not only deny *them,* but Spirits; and are obliquely and upon consequence a sort not of Infidels, but Atheists.[14]

Lady Macbeth calling the witches "fate and metaphysical aid"

(1.5.29) begins clearly in such disbelief, despite her own attempts to assimilate the power of evil in her person. She is troubled by the resemblance of Duncan to her father, but she sees no ghosts and sneers at Macbeth's visions, until far into the play.

> This is the very painting of your fear.
> This is the air-drawn dagger which you said
> Led you to Duncan. O, these flaws and starts
> (Impostors to true fear) would well become
> A woman's story at a winter's fire,
> Authorized by her grandam. Shame itself!
> Why do you make such faces?
>
> (3.4.76–82)

"Out, damned spot! out, I say!" is her punishment not only for being an accomplice to murder, but also specifically for this denial of ghosts. Macbeth's plea to the doctor to cure his wife of her conscience, "the very painting" of her "fear," tolls ironic in the play. "Canst thou not minister to a mind diseased" (5.3.47) is specious considering his own belief, his fear that murder risks "the life to come." It is not disease Macbeth knows but conscience that has struck his wife. Lady Macbeth warns her husband of the consequence if she has to "Consider . . . so deeply" the murder (2.2.43) that "These deeds must not be thought / After these ways. So, it will make us mad" (2.2.47–48). Belief in her brings madness, in Macbeth, only further despair.

Time disappears for Macbeth, in the wake of his crime—future time, that is—its symptom that he either can not sleep, or fears to. This recalls Hamlet's line of self-reflection on suicide: "For in that sleep of death, what dreams may come" (FF.3.1: 1720). It is piteous that the Thane, a man fixed in reflection on time, should cheat himself of future time. It will finally estrange Macbeth from his wife, who begs him to enjoy the present. At the beginning of the play, steeped in battle weariness and frightened of what his thoughts portend for the future, Macbeth still praises time: "Come what come may, / Time and the hour runs through the roughest day" (1.3.164–65). When his wife taunts him "beguile the time, / Look like the time;" just after she has abused "This ignorant present" and claimed to "feel now / The future in the instant" (1.5.71–72, 62, and 63), she is juggling in the same way that Macbeth tried to "beguile" himself as to whether murder would "jump the life to come." Macbeth's soliloquy that opens scene 7 of the first act begins as an attempt to picture outracing the deed by doing it quickly. He tries to imagine a way in which the murder's consequences will not work themselves out in time. He breaks off from these reflections by reminding himself of the horror of the crime itself, but these inevitably return him to future time and judgment. "This is the time," Lady Macbeth screams at him in so many words: "Nor time nor place / Did then adhere, and yet you would make them both. / They have made themselves, and that their fitness now / Does unmake you" (1.7.57–60). Time has raced ahead in her imagination, but she understands that her husband is badly frightened and forces him to return to the past, his ruminations on the crown, in order to act in the present. The triple repetition, "make," "made," "unmake," strike like hammer blows at Macbeth's manhood, but they also confuse his sense of time. His conclusion to the scene between Lady Macbeth and himself echoes of self-knowledge: "Away, and mock the time with fairest show" (1.7.92). It is not the present to which Lady Macbeth has returned her husband, but the future that she has bound to the present, "in the instant" not understanding her action's import. This is what mocks Macbeth even as he pretends to mock the present. It is the future, the subject of his first reflections in the scene, that is the underlying bitter matter of its last couplet. Macbeth tries to pretend to a clear face when all is now cloudy, and time lost. Surely this is what "the false heart doth know."

Time in the play will beat about Macbeth's head like madness. The references are legion, the most famous being, "Tomorrow, and tomorrow, and tomorrow" (5.5.21), when there is for him, no tomorrow. There is no "hereafter" in which to mourn Lady Macbeth, either literally, since he must go out to battle, or in a spiritual life where it would have meaning. Time like Banquo's line of children, exists now only to mock Macbeth. Yet his bold words about time's lack of meaning, will be undercut by his superstitious dread at the words of Macduff.

The nihilism that dogs King Lear, signified in the word "nothing," rises to king of Scotland's lips as the latter's end draws near.

> Life's but a walking shadow, a poor player,
> That struts and frets his hour upon the stage
> And then is heard no more. It is a tale
> Told by an idiot, full of sound and fury,
> Signifying nothing.

> (5.5.26–30)

Is it the playwright speaking, in the absolute despair, that his work and life is just that, idiotic and meaningless? The contempt

of Malcolm at the end for the torment of despair that has gone
before, speaking of the two protagonists as "this dead butcher and
his fiendlike queen," is only a further expression of this "self-
abuse."

What could have brought Shakespeare, his tragic hero, and
heroine to such a bleak conclusion? If there is an answer in the
play, surely it is the riddle propounded by the witches as the
drama began.

> Lesser than Macbeth, and greater.
> Not so happy, yet much happier.
>
> (1.3.70–71)

Speaking this with a sarcastic riddling, the witches nevertheless
define what Shakespeare considers happiness, when it comes to
ambition, whether in war, politics, or literature. This is the not so
apparent theme of the play, deliberately concealed in its murky
twilight. It will appear at first that the getting of the supreme temporal position, i.e., the crown, is happiness, but in fact it will be
the bequeathing of a crown to one's children that is the definition
for the witches (the "much happier") and one can presume, for
Shakespeare, their puppeteer, of happiness, which is here equated
as indivisible from ambition. Macbeth is warned at the very beginning that he will be cheated of the object of his ambition even in
the getting of it. This is a kind of cruelty that has not been observed
either in *Hamlet* or *King Lear*. Neither father or daughters speak
about the sadness of their line dying out in *Lear*, nor do Ghost or
Prince show any concern on this theme in *Hamlet*, though in both
tragedies this is an obvious conclusion. Yet it is not admitted as
part of the action's pathos. Such pathos is paramount in *Macbeth*
and speaks to the melancholy of the playwright, cheated of a direct
male heir, feeling the loss of his son, and of Shakespeare's country,
England, experiencing the end of the Tudor dynasty.[15]

7

What Prospero Knows

THE Tempest is above all about control, control of the primitive and the spiritual, the base and the refined, personified by Caliban and Ariel. It is based on the same question—revenge—as Hamlet, but now its hero will be in complete control of the situation. The audience's ignorance of Prospero's knowledge will create the illusion of a threat, never will he be threatened in fact. Hamlet can never control his situation, the plot he finds himself embroiled in. Prospero on the other hand both creates and manipulates the plot, play. All the anxiety of a playwright whose plot is escaping from him, defying him, gives a background of dissonance, modern music, to the events of *Hamlet*. *The Tempest* by contrast is baroque, an anticipation of the eighteenth century, the work of a playwright supremely confident, even a trifle bored.

This is *The Tempest* as it appears in a superficial performance or a first reading. Closer attention reveals a play of deep anxiety—which may answer the question of why so much in the plot is left unresolved.[1] It is not the characters who interest Prospero, or Shakespeare—with the exception perhaps of Miranda, and by extension Caliban, who may stand for the father's buried sexual life—but time and dream. The revenge is a comedy, the play outside a "play" in which Prospero has been acting—absorbed in the world of his books, his thoughts of death. The latter—the play of the sorcerer's mind—may be the drama that Shakespeare has wryly called "The Tempest." What is in that *library*, that *book*, which Prospero "drowns." A passing dukedom in Milan is trivia to a man who can command wind, waves, illusion. Why then is the sorcerer so melancholy, angry? What is the "tempest" in his head? There are only flitting glances of this interior world, which Prospero has told Miranda is so important that it distracted him from his own dukedom and its opportunities for power.

Prospero is a man caught in time who desires to be beyond it. Despite the wizard's magic, his sleights of hand, it is all temporal,

dependent as he himself admits on the junction of faraway stars.
He has but an instant to act, or he and his opportunity will be lost.

> . . . by my prescience
> I find my zenith doth depend upon
> A most auspicious star, whose influence
> If now I court not, but omit, my fortunes
> Will ever after droop.
>
> (1.2.180–84)

His moment, does not alter, however, Prospero's own predica-
ment. Despite books, staff, such magic is superficial. The play itself will be the sorcerer's "zenith," his summit or highest point.
What lies beyond? Is there nothing higher toward which Prospero
may aspire? Is there just a touch of pessimism in that "zenith"?
Overarching the sorcerer is the greater mystery, time. Yes, he has
mastered perhaps the most feared of the wizard's feats, the resurrection of the dead:

> . . . graves at my command
> Have waked their sleepers, oped, and let 'em forth
> By my so potent art. But this rough magic
> I here abjure,

Such resurrection is but "rough magic," like his feats of drawing
down thunder, lightning, rain. Why should it be so? His magical
craft's exact limits are never made clear. The sorcerer's obsession,
time, keeps breaking in on him. It draws one of those peculiar
lines that speak of Prospero's emotions in *The Tempest*, lines that
contradict the tenor of the scene and speech in which he speaks
them. So, at the beginning of what ought to be a factual exposition
of Prospero's history and Miranda's, his portentous apothegm
there is "In the dark backward and abysm of time."

Why the sudden darkening of metaphor, speaking of time? The
answer is complex. Miranda's ability to remember events at the
edge of memory, gives her a power akin to sorcery, which looks
forward and backward in time. Within their short exchange, Prospero is suddenly aroused to curiosity, then relieved at the limitations of his daughter's "remembrance."

> . . . Canst thou remember
> A time before we came into this cell?
> I do not think thou canst, for then thou wast not
> Out three years old.

Miranda. Certainly, sir, I can.
Prospero. By what? By any other house or person?
  Of any thing the image tell me, that
  Hath kept with thy remembrance.
Miranda. 'Tis far off,
  And rather like a dream than an assurance
  That my remembrance warrants. Had I not
  Four or five women once that tended me?
Prospero. Thou hadst, and more, Miranda. But how is it
  That this lives in thy mind? What seest thou else
  In the dark backward and abysm of time?
  If thou rememb'rest aught ere thou cam'st here,
  How thou cam'st here thou mayst.
Miranda. But that I do not.

(1.2.38–52)

To Prospero's patronizing, "I do not think thou canst," Miranda sharply replies, "Certainly, sir, I can." This ought to be a shock, both to the father and to the audience. It suggests that there are many mysteries in Miranda's consciousness that the wizard is not in control of. His ability to see is limited, and his daughter has a gift of sight too. "How is it that this lives in thy mind?" is an admission of Miranda's independence on her father's part, mingling wonder and realization. Will she be a sharer in his knowledge? The next line broaches that question, the "abysm," but then Prospero makes his next query specific. He asks only if she remembers how she came to the island? Is he skirting the implications of the "dark backward"? Other shadowy images may be there as well. Prospero receives, it seems almost gratefully, the reassurance that Miranda knows nothing of their flight and hurries on to tell her of details of their leaving Milan. Of that terror, at least, she has no buried phantoms. (I have been at pains to go over the passage line by line because in its transparent exposition, two emotional and metaphysical questions of *The Tempest* are defined, Miranda's innocence, Prospero's anxiety.)

Under Prospero's queries to Miranda about her memory, her sense of time, and his daughter's guileless replies runs information of a dangerous hothouse confinement. She has been sequestered with her father in his cell on the island since she can remember. What vague impressions she has of creatures in the time before are of women not men. Miranda makes this explicit. She tells Ferdinand that she has seen no other men: "Nor have I seen / More that I may call men than you, good friend, / And my dear father" (3.1.50–52). Prospero has encouraged Miranda's innocence, sens-

ing perhaps her natural repulsion to Caliban, whom she understands is not human. The sorcerer rightly fears, however, that
faced with a real man she will be in danger, especially as Miranda
demonstrates a mind of her own. The comedy will mask the
strangeness of what transpires and Prospero's ambiguous role. Miranda worships the first man she sees. Caliban, in robust comic
parallel, recognizes the first and second men he comes upon as
"sprites." For the sake of the "celestial liquor," the monster is prepared to worship too and hails the drunken Stephano as a "brave
god" (2.2.115). The audience hears the echo of Miranda's wonder
as she gazes on Ferdinand, "What is't? A spirit?" and her observation of this male "spirit" that "It carries a brave form" (1.2.410 and
412). How dangerous Miranda's naiveté might be is suggested in
her exclamation beholding the court of Naples. Miranda's enthusiasm does not distinguish between good and evil:

> O, wonder!
> How many goodly creatures are there here!
> How beauteous mankind is! O brave new world,
> That has such people in't!

It prompts Prospero's sardonic, "'Tis new to thee" (5.1.181–84).

While at first breath, it is *Hamlet* that *The Tempest* suggests with
questions of control, anxiety, a younger brother's will to usurp an
older brother's kingdom, clearly the riddle of *King Lear,* a father's
love for a much younger daughter is *The Tempest's* storm center.
Prospero in effect realizes the fantasy of Lear, to be locked away in
a cell with his daughter, the bed of "Incense," strewn by the gods.[2]
The dangers of this lead Shakespeare to describe a puritan up-
bringing. Prospero represents himself "austerely" to Ferdinand
(4.1.1). Miranda has entered into her father's cell not in the bloom
of maidenhood, as Cordelia does, but at the edge of infancy when
nothing can clearly be remembered. The very day, however, on
which all is revealed, Miranda leaves. Otherwise the incestuous
space of which Lear dreams, "Birds i'th'Cage,"[3] must develop.
Shakespeare admits the pull of the incestuous in *Hamlet,* where
the young man's repugnance to his father's murder gives his sexual
imagination license in regard to his mother. Hamlet's anger in performance distracts from the danger of his stewing in details of his
mother's lovemaking, a catalogue that reveals his fascination, and
suggests that the choice of the clearly adolescent Ophelia may be
a blind to his own attraction to the powerful sexual stimulus of
Gertrude.

Prospero will call his daughter "wench" three times. It is a peculiar word and can run the gamut of meaning in Elizabethan usage from affection to contempt. It might well be interpreted as a father's innocent epithet, but the audience has heard it before it comes to Prospero's mouth. The ship, cries the pious but salty Gonzalo, in the pitching sea of the first scene, is "as leaky as an / unstanched wench" (1.1.46–47). This image of a woman in orgasm pouring out juices as she calls for more satisfaction sets the tone for subsequent usage. When Prospero in the next scene addresses Miranda with the epithet, it will echo of the inn and brothel, a strange familiarity. "Well demanded, wench!" (1.2.139), responds the father as Miranda begins to question him about their banishment; "No, wench. It eats and sleeps and hath such senses / As we have, such" (1.2.413–14). In this last, the sexual interest is plain, since Prospero's rival for Miranda, Ferdinand, is approaching. The "it" is humorous, obviously referring to the beast, Caliban, in which category Prospero teasingly has put the "gallant" to Miranda's dissatisfaction, for she is instantly attracted to Ferdinand. Her cry of protest, "I might call him / A *thing* divine!" banters Prospero's "it," but also justifies her father's "wench." This reference to Caliban in the "it" is made specific (in 1.2.479–81) where the third "wench" occurs: "Thou think'st there is no more such shapes as he, / Having seen but him and Caliban. Foolish wench! / To th'most of men this is a Caliban . . . ." The epithet "wench" is the more surprising because we know that Miranda has laid eyes on no real man but her father, and that Caliban's approach has appalled her. It will echo sardonically in Antonio's mock at the island's climate: "Temperance was a delicate wench" (2.1.46). The last stresses "wench"'s sexual implications. Climate is notoriously changeable, and "wench" in this context carries the implication of an inevitable fall from virtue.

Prospero's use of "wench" suggests that not only is the sorcerer's magic "rough" but his character as well. There is a death in Prospero, which echoes the offstage death of that "piece of virtue" (an almost ugly phrase), his wife. He looks forward to no new allegiances, no new children, no sexual life although he seems young enough and vigorous. Why?

The answer (I imagine) is simple. It is what has cost him his kingdom—his studies, his books. It is no idle gesture then, when, at the end of the play, Prospero flings his book, his art away. The image is quite specific. His staff will be buried, "certain fathoms in the earth" (the nautical measure is suggestive of what is to come), but his written material "deeper than did ever plummet sound / I'll drown my book" (5.1.56–57).

The passage summons a curious train of what Reuben Brower has called the "continuities" and "analogies" of *The Tempest*, images that appear repetitively and give the play structure. Brower, however, reads the play optimistically, and, therefore, the clouds of its storm are quickly dispelled. I, alas, hear quite a different pattern. (See pp. 131–32.)

Stephen Greenblatt[4] has pointed out the deliberate use of anxiety by Prospero to heighten the sense of fear and trembling in his adversaries, to cause them to convert, to experience a moral reawakening. Prospero himself is a creature of anxiety.[5] It is easy to attribute his ugliness, his harshness, to *senex*, the type of the Roman drama on which much of the plot is obviously based.[6] (The obvious *senex* of *The Tempest* is Gonzalo, who is remarkably sweet-tempered in what may be a deliberate comparison.) There is some distance between irritability and anxiety. Like King Lear, Prospero is not merely quick-tempered, he is frightened. Lear's favorite daughter's, Cordelia's, reply of "nothing" in the game the monarch, "Unburthen'd" crawling "toward death" proposes in the first act of *King Lear*, sets loose a reaction that neither Lear nor Cordelia anticipate. "Nothing" touches precisely on King Lear's deepest fears—and that fear links *King Lear* to *The Tempest*. King Lear begins fearing his own death and ends by dying, broken-hearted at his daughter's. Prospero, while obviously doting on Miranda's reactions, is more balanced. The sorcerer's anxiety is divided, as he will inform us, a third for death, a third for his daughter, a third presumably for everything, everyone, else.

Shakespeare has been unusually devious, however, in revealing Prospero to the audience. The sorcerer's concern for Miranda is deciphered in his double, Alonso, king of Naples. The terror in *The Tempest* is emphasized by the way the fathers in this play dote on their children. Alonso wants to lie down in the same bed as his son, Ferdinand, below the waves.

It is a strange image—to be "mudded" that Alonso uses, following the sexual "bedded." It emphasizes the opposition of death and sex and their common confounding in creation. The word "ooze" is the treacherous firmament of *The Tempest*. It is the sea bed. It is also, in a striking pun, the marriage bed. Caliban just a few moments before King Alonso speaks of being bedded in the mud, has promised Stephano that Miranda, "will become thy bed . . . / And bring thee forth brave brood" (3.2.105–6). Alonso, Prospero's only equal in the play, a shadow to the sorcerer, sinks deeper and deeper into melancholy. Ferdinand's presumed death in the sea brings Alonso to the image of ooze, but it is the echo of Prospero's voice that calls it up.

> . . . the thunder,
> That deep and dreadful organ-pipe, pronounced
> The name of Prosper: it did bass my trespass.
> Therefore my son i'th'ooze is bedded, and
> I'll seek him deeper than e'er plummet sounded,
> And with him there lie mudded.
>
> (3.3.99–104)

Alonso repeats this making it even more specific: "I wish / Myself were mudded in that oozy bed / Where my son lies" (5.1. 150–52). Since the "oozy bed" where Ferdinand will lie is Miranda's, this is a flirtation with incest on Shakespeare's part. Prospero has earlier mentioned the dark bog under the sea, akin to the primeval chaos, reminiscent of a world before time: "think'st it much to tread the ooze / Of the salt deep" (1.2. 252–53), and even the spiritual Ariel sings of it.

Magic creates this miasmal swamp, this chaos, and, as the characters rise from it, Prospero calls out, "Their understanding / Begins to swell, and the approaching tide / Will shortly fill the reasonable shore / That now lies foul and muddy." This primeval ooze, beyond time, is the resting place of the most fearful object in the play, Prospero's book, consigned below the seabed, as the metaphor makes clear, "certain fathoms in the earth, / And deeper than did ever plummet sound."

The comic characters too, wallow in the surface of ooze. Ariel leads them into a bog, "th'filthy mantled pool beyond your cell, / There dancing up to th'chins, that the foul lake / O'erstunk their feet" (4.1.182–84). Trinculo exclaims, "Monster, I do smell all horse-piss, at which / my nose is in great indignation" (4.1.199–200). Caliban, a "fish" in appearance, or rather a fish that crawls upon the land, is a creature of the bog, the miasma, the confusion. It is from this realm that Caliban calls up his curse on Prospero.

> All the infections that the sun sucks up
> From bogs, fens, flats, on Prosper fall. . . .
>
> (2.2.1–2)

Even Ariel's famous song, read in this key, is ominous: "Full fathom five thy father lies. . . ." Brower speaks of this "sea change" as "Shakespeare's most direct expression of his key metaphor. . . . But what does Shakespeare mean by 'sea change'? Ariel sings of 'bones' being made into 'coral' and of 'eyes' becoming 'pearls.' 'A change into something rich and strange,' we now understand is a change 'out of nature.' 'Sea change' is a metaphor for 'magical transformation,' for metamorphosis. The key metaphor of the play is 'change' in this special sense, and 'change' is the analogy common to all the continuities we have been tracing."[7] With all due respect to a beloved teacher, I must disagree—not so much with the idea of change as the key metaphor, but with the sanguine tone that runs under the reading. It is, after all, a song of death—expressed in "rich and strange" metaphor—but that does not alter the reality of a dead man lying ossified into coral and pearl. Ariel as a spirit may speak of such a change as marvelous, magical, but Ferdinand can hardly be comforted. I suggest reading the lines in a mocking voice for that is exactly what they do, tease and mock Ferdinand's grief.

> Full fathom five thy father lies,
> Of his bones are coral made;
> Those are pearls that were his eyes;
> Nothing of him that doth fade,
> But doth suffer a sea-change
> Into something rich and strange.
> Sea-nymphs hourly ring his knell:
> (Burden) Ding-dong.
> Hark! Now I hear them—Ding-dong bell.

The eerie sound of the chorus of spirits going "ding-dong" in parody of a church bell, a harbor bell, to a Ferdinand presumably beside himself at the loss of a father is a kind of teasing. The audience will hear and see this mockery of death again when Prospero, punning on the word "loss," will pretend to Alonso in act 5, scene 1, that he has lost a child too. It is funny but cruel and smacks of the comic revenge of Milan on Naples—for the "ding-dong" tolls death. The "sea-change" may be marvelous, but so may death be. The audience's laughter must be rather anxious—for they are not so sure of it. Yet this is "the rich and strange" world to which Prospero himself is sailing throughout *The Tempest*.

* * *

One of the problems of the play in production, which most critics prefer to ignore, is the inattention of Miranda in act 1, scene 2. Three times she is scolded about not listening. Does she in fact lapse in attention, or is this only a curious device to wake up an audience that must suffer a particularly long exposition? If we recognize Prospero is creating anxiety, then we must wonder if it is always for moral conversion. Is he not expressing his own anxiety? Is he not, in fact, enjoying its expression and wanting to feel it in his daughter.

Miranda cries. Countless lines in the play testify to the fact that she cries easily and often. Prospero wants those tears for himself, for the tears are a form of sexual endearment from his daughter and a sublimation of their mutual attraction. She cries for the people on the boat, the first humans she has seen since she was three years old—and those but dimly remembered. In Prospero's eyes she is crying for a boat mostly full of drunken sailors, varlets, and villains. Those tears are properly a father's as far as Prospero is concerned, and not until Miranda cries out that she must have been a burden to Prospero, not until she abandons her thoughts of the ship crew and indeed enters "the dark backward and abysm of time" to dwell in her childhood again, does the wizard relent and show his tenderness. She will cry to her father in compassion, guilt, self reproach, "Alack, what trouble / Was I then to you!"

This draws in return Prospero's full-hearted admission of love; "O, a cherubin / Thou wast that did preserve me. Thou didst smile, / Infusèd with a fortitude from heaven, / When I have decked the sea with drops full salt . . . ." I would suggest that, in fact, Prospero weeps as he says it, weeps taking Miranda into his arms again, reliving the moment, and since she is weeping from the beginning of the act, obviously they weep and embrace together.

The scene dramatizes a Prospero locked into his own thoughts, living back in time, who, when he looks up to the present, is amazed to see his daughter sitting as a spectator, not as a party suffering it again. Not until she suffers and cries out to him can he be released from his bondage to this time. This will be demonstrated again in the sudden interruption of the masque he presents to his Miranda and Ferdinand. He is a man absorbed in his dreams, his own thoughts, and, as a sorcerer, he withdraws into that realm and acts from it. To the outsider, it seems like a form of possession not action—for this is the metier of all magic.

What are these thoughts? A third of them, even when Prospero returns to busy Milan will be about death—that he assures the audience. On the island, where he has time on his hands, it can not be less. A third accompany his daughter—and another third— on the almost idyllic island, controlled by his books, I suggest— involve the idyll itself. It is no accident then that Gonzalo, landing on the island, begins to imagine a Utopia. Ferdinand's highest compliment to Prospero's, his future father-in-law's, magical prowess, encompasses this.

> Let me live here ever!
> So rare a wondered father and a wise
> Makes this place Paradise.
>
> (4.1.122–24)

What is the quality of paradise, as Shakespeare and we, his inheritors in the West, would imagine it in the wake of the biblical stories? I would say innocence. Man is innocent in the Garden. In a strange twist, it is woman who is innocent in *The Tempest*. To maintain this innocence before inevitable temptation, his own, hers, Ferdinand's, is one of the struggles of Prospero. If he can not do it, the idyll, the Paradise he has created, will come crashing down upon his ears. Therefore the sorcerer's obsession with Miranda's chastity, his sermon about her marriage bed:

> If thou dost break her virgin-knot before
> All sanctimonious ceremonies may
> With full and holy rite be ministered,
> No sweet aspersion shall the heavens let fall
> To make this contract grow; but barren hate,
> Sour-eyed disdain and discord shall bestrew
> The union of your bed with weeds so loathly
> That you shall hate it both. Therefore take heed,
> As Hymen's lamps shall light you.
>
> (4.1.15–23)

Therefore the danger of her absolute surrender to Ferdinand in terms that are a flirtation with disaster.

The sweetness of her voice in part disguises her offer.

> . . . How features are abroad
> I am skill-less of; but, by my modesty,
> The jewel in my dower, I would not wish
> Any companion in the world but you.
> Nor can imagination form a shape,
> Beside yourself, to like of.
>
> (3.1.52–57)

"Jewel," an allusion to "chastity incarnate in the maidenhead,"[8] makes clear that Miranda, in mentioning her virginity, swearing on it that she wishes only his companionship, is offering it. This is made explicit a few moments on, as they exchange love vows and Miranda begins, predictably, to weep. Ferdinand, quite naturally, is alarmed, but, to his "Wherefore weep you?" Miranda artfully first protests that she must hide and "dare not offer," but then does indeed "offer" using as Anne Righter points out, the image of "a secret pregnancy." The critic is so embarrassed by it, she protests, "Sexual allusion of this kind hardly seems appropriate to Miranda. . . ."[9] On the contrary, sexual allusion, is what this scene is all about. Miranda will call it "plain and holy innocence" to state that either as wife or "maid," the latter not quite as bald as "wench," but still carrying some ambivalence in its meaning, she will follow him about. "I'll be your servant," i.e., I am your slave, she says. Of course, Ferdinand has played and will play with this theme too, willing "bondage," but it has a very different force coming from a virgin's mouth.

> . . . mine unworthiness, that dare not offer
> What I desire to give, and much less take
> What I shall die to want. But this is trifling;
> And all the more it seeks to hide itself,
> The bigger bulk it shows. Hence, bashful cunning!
> And prompt me, plain and holy innocence.
> I am your wife, if you will marry me.
> If not, I'll die your maid. To be your fellow
> You may deny me, but I'll be your servant
> Whether you will or no.
>
> (3.1.77–86)

* * *

Many critics have noted the references throughout the play to Utopia, and editions of *The Tempest* often include several probable sources for Shakespeare's meditations on Paradise: William Strachey's "True Repertory of the Wrack," Sylvester Jourdain's "A Discovery of the Barmudas" the report of the Council of Virginia, "The True Declaration of the Estate of the Colony in Virginia," and Michel de Montaigne's "Of the Cannibals." The one direct description of Utopia, Gonzalo's, in act 2, scene 1, lines 150–59 and 162–67, is almost deliberately naive.

> I'th'commonwealth I would by contraries
> Execute all things. For no kind of traffic
> Would I admit, no name of magistrate.
> Letters should not be known. Riches, poverty,
> And use of service, none. Contract, succession,
> Bourn, bound of land, tilth, vineyard, none.

No use of metal, corn, or wine, or oil.
No occupation: all men idle, all,
And women too, but innocent and pure.
No sovereignty—. . . .
All things in common nature should produce
Without sweat or endeavor. Treason, felony,
Sword, pike, knife, gun, or need of any engine
Would I not have; but nature should bring forth
Of it own kind all foison, all abundance,
To feed my innocent people.

Sebastian mocks Gonzalo out of the side of his mouth with, "No marrying 'mong his / subjects?" and draws Antonio's sarcastic rejoinder, "None, man, all idle—whores / and knaves." There is some justification in the raillery, for Gonzalo's utopia exceeds the possibilities even of the rich Bermudas, where the earth, sea, air, seemed to the shipwrecked English sailors to give bounty without effort. In fact, Gonzalo is describing a world beyond the real one—Paradise. It is a word that Ferdinand will utter in the thrall of Prospero's magic, convinced that the island is identical to it: "Let me live here ever! . . . this place Paradise."

Miranda's innocence as well suggests the Garden of Eden before the Fall. Shakespeare is asking in *The Tempest* what kind of a paradise human beings might imagine. The island paradise is illusion, but Prospero wonders if the stuff of life is not illusion too. He is a master at manipulating illusion yet he is equally subject to it and helpless before it, and powerless, for even his book belongs to that ooze or sea change as Ariel transforms it, the realm of death. It is a death haunted play, not entirely melancholy, because Prospero is able to give it over to the young lovers, Ferdinand and Miranda, make his final act of art, a masque for their wedding celebration.

Freedom and slavery, Caliban's song, "Freedom, high-day! High-day, freedom! Freedom, / high-day, freedom!" (2.2.182–83), is followed by the slavery of Ferdinand to love. Literally in the next line, act 3, scene 1, Ferdinand enters bearing a log. Love is indeed the only redemption from the slavery of time, of death, and Prospero's only object, Miranda, is forbidden to him. The sorcerer's line, giving away his daughter, continues to echo, ambiguously, after it has been spoken: "I / Have given you here a third of mine own life, / Or that for which I live" (4.1.2–4). Is Miranda a third of what he lives for or *all* that he lives for? If all, a very melancholy man indeed is revealed. In the world at least, if so, Prospero's illusions are behind him. Only his daughter is before him. If this be translated into Shakespeare's biography, the audience glimpses, for a moment, the sadness of the playwright as he leaves the stage for Stratford and whatever happiness his daughters' lives may bring his own.

*   *   *

I began with a discussion of time. Many critics have noted its importance in the play. Righter remarks:

> More promising, perhaps, than any attempt to explain *The Tempest* by way of its sources is the question of its adherence to the classical unities of time, place, and action. This is a straightforward fact about the play, and one of enormous importance. Here, for some reason, Shakespeare chose to contradict the practice of a lifetime and construct a drama according to neo-classical principles . . . . On two important occasions in *The Tempest*, Prospero inquires the time from Ariel. In the first instance, in Act 1, his question serves to indicate how long he expects the action to take: "The time 'twixt six and now / Must by us both be spent most preciously" (1.2.240–41). The second, at the beginning of Act 5, assures the audience that he is indeed accomplishing his purposes within the span of time allotted for them (5.1.4–5).[10]

The critic goes on to point out the many other instances of emphasis on time. Shakespeare lay such emphasis on time because the tragedy of time, as well as its sad comedy, is what *The Tempest* is about.

One of the striking oddities of *The Tempest* is the way minor characters, villainous ones at that, are given piquant lines. Trinculo's "Misery acquaints a man with strange bed-fellows" is a comic example. The most eloquent speech about dream is naturally Prospero's, questioning the reality of life.

. . . We are such stuff
As dreams are made on; and our little life
Is rounded with a sleep.

(4.1.156–58)

Yet its sentiments are echoed by Sebastian, though perhaps unconsciously. Still the latter's words might well be appended to Prospero's apostrophe to the condition of life, the puzzle of consciousness: "This is a strange repose, to be asleep / With eyes wide open; standing, speaking, moving, / And yet so fast asleep" (2.1.217–19). Sebastian and Antonio are under the charm of Prospero, but in fact they are suddenly in the presence of their murderous fantasies, which, one might convincingly argue, is their true reality and a description of their state, when quite awake to themselves. Again the play returns the audience in a minor key to the riddle of time, consciousness, death. Prospero can certainly echo, Sebastian's, "It is a sleepy language, and thou speak'st / Out of thy sleep."

The verses recall Samuel Daniel's sonnet, "Care-charmer sleep, son of the sable night / Brother to death, in silent darkness born," and its final couplet, "Still let me sleep, embracing clouds in vain, / And never wake to feel the day's disdain." This is very close to Caliban's

> Sometimes a thousand twangling instruments
> Will hum about mine ears; and sometime voices
> That, if I then had waked after long sleep,
> Will make me sleep again; and then, in dreaming,
> The clouds methought would open, and show riches
> Ready to drop upon me, that when I waked
> I cried to dream again.

This wish to abandon reality for the richness of dream makes the bestial servant one with his master. It suggests also another realm, "that sleep of death" which previously Hamlet, for one, had feared: "To sleep, perchance to Dream; / I, there's the rub, / For in that sleep of death, what dreams may come, / When we have shuffl'd off this mortal coil." Prospero, whose every third thought will be death, seems to indicate that he anticipates this promised land, this final utopia. Sleep and dream lie ahead as a foretaste of Paradise, even for poor, base Caliban. It is precisely because a captain like Macbeth can not sleep, steeped in blood, can not look forward to sleep, that his tragedy is more awful than King Lear's or Prince Hamlet's. Macbeth feels damned. There is no "life to come," to leap toward from "this bank and shoal of time,"[11] for him. The most precious time, Shakespeare muses, lies beyond human time.

And yet? And yet? The speech in which Prospero breaks up the show within the show, the spirits' drama, is the real farewell of the play—a farewell to life, not an appeal for clapping from a live audience. "Be cheerful sir. / Our revels now are ended," has a bittersweet taste, even to Ferdinand, who becomes dismayed with Miranda, seeing Prospero's face gripped by some nameless fury. Why should the trivial plot of Caliban work the sorcerer into a "passion / That works him strongly," so much so that Miranda will cry out, "Never till this day / Saw I him touched with anger so distempered."

Prospero is not aware of what his face shows. He turns to Ferdinand, sees that the latter is frightened, and immediately becomes genial.

> You do look, my son, in a moved sort,
> As if you were dismayed. Be cheerful, sir.
> Our revels now are ended. These our actors,
> As I foretold you, were all spirits, and
> Are melted into air, into thin air;
> And, like the baseless fabric of this vision,
> The cloud-capped towers, the gorgeous palaces,
> The solemn temples, the great globe itself,
> Yea, all which it inherit, shall dissolve,
> And, like this insubstantial pageant faded,
> Leave not a rack behind. We are such stuff . . .

It is not the pageant that has "dismayed" Ferdinand, but Prospero's face. The quick turn of emotions, the sorcerer's misunderstanding, may indeed be funny on the stage, yet they point again to anxiety to which the comedy does not entirely admit. While I may demur at the notion of a formal religious conversion (see note 5), still I can not entirely dismiss the idea of a crisis of faith running under the events of *The Tempest* for Prospero, and by extension, Shakespeare. The critic who notes the sorcerer's sudden breaking off of the masque of fertility, autumn, spring, to address the plot of his life, has touched on a puzzle that the play refuses to directly clarify. It is, however, precisely after the line "sunburned sicklemen, of August weary, / Come hither from the furrow, and be merry. . . ," as the dance of the reapers begins, even in "holiday," that Prospero starts. The sickle suggests time, the reaper, death. The joyous "country footing" of "the fresh nymphs" and the sicklemen in "rye-straw hats" suggest to the sorcerer in middle age something very different than they do to the young lovers.

Sleep, dream, innocence, utopia—are they behind the conjurer, or before him? Prospero says good-bye, and through him Shakespeare, three times in *The Tempest*. He bids the audience farewell in the speech "Our revels now are ended" when he brings the pageant to a close. Again, he bids farewell when he promises to break his staff and bury his book. He does so finally at the conclusion of the play itself. Prospero and his playwright, speaking through the magician, are looking to a world beyond, a place to which book, staff, craft, can not bring either the, oozy bed on which, in which, Shakespeare senses he soon will lie.[12]

8

Shakespeare's Myth

SHAKESPEARE—was it Hazlitt who invented the faceless Shakespeare? "We have been so used to this tragedy [*Hamlet*] that we hardly know how to criticize it any more than we should know how to describe our own faces."[1] Borges romanticized it even further. Why did this myth take root; was it because somehow the effect of the work was so profound, mysterious that there was a desire to deify—which one can see in Boccaccio's treatment of Dante—to erase the man and leave a peacock under a tree. This impulse has led to many theories of other authors for the plays. But why seek to evade Shakespeare? He had somehow hit, as Sophocles had, as had Hesiod or Hesiod's redactor, or Homer or Homer's redactor, on the myths of a culture, and William Shakespeare found himself swept up in the mythology. (The Bible, aware of this tendency, that is, man's desire to mythologize a great human teacher, in the biography of Moses argues a historical Moses, for Moses refuses to let himself be mythologized in death.)

The effort to give Shakespeare's biography to another, make it a mystery, founders on the presence of too many scraps, papers, records, that give the playwright from Stratford an objective existence. One does not look for Sophocles' biography in *Oedipus Rex*, despite the grim truth of the play. We do look for a Hesiod and a Homer in their work, but of course the former is named, while the latter flashes before us in the persona of the bards who sing and in Odysseus's own skill in narration, stepping forward in the palace of the Phaiakians to sing many lines of his own epic. Yet critics are uneasy at the idea of a biography of Hesiod or Homer drawn from the poems.[2]

Shakespeare does not name himself, nor do playwrights appear in his work (although over and over, Hamlet, Lear, and Prospero are busy staging dramas, and Macbeth at the end can not draw a line between reality and a player acting, badly, it seems, in a bad play). Shakespeare, however, has expressed so powerfully the collective secular nightmares that are the source of modern myth that, like the poet, or poets, who composed *The Iliad, The Odyssey, The Theogony,* Shakespeare seems to be describing not fiction or poetry, but the world as it *was* and unriddling for us what *is* now and what is to be. The fear of the father eating his children, the mother plotting to castrate the father with the help of her children, the incestuous unions with sisters, wives, daughters, sons, all of which Hesiod names, are equally present in Shakespeare but without gods as the looming ogres.

The strong oedipal feelings in *Hamlet,* the Prince's attraction to his mother, the buried resentment of the past father, which is a riddle, the obvious and open anger toward the present usurper, Claudius, are clichés of Shakespearian criticism. What is not obvious, perhaps, is why Shakespeare would have been attracted to the situation, in the treatment of which he differs radically from Sophocles. It is relevant to ask, indeed, what makes Sophocles' drama of conflict between generations so different from Hesiod's, one of the Greek playwright's sources. The *Theogony* of Hesiod makes it obvious why Sophocles' genius would guide him to Oedipus. Oedipus slays the Sphinx, who is the child of an incestuous union between a mother, Echidna, half woman and half snake, and her son Orchus. (Echidna herself is the daughter of the incest between a sister, "fair cheeked" Ceto and a brother, Phorcys, both the children of Pontus, "the fruitless deep with his raging swell" the son of Gaia by parthenogenesis.) Incest is a given of Greek divinity. If such divinity is a human projection, as some critics insist, it touches our raw, private speculations about birth, love, family tragedy.

In the eyes of the Sphinx, Oedipus, after his expulsion from Thebes, would be no monster, rather a kindred spirit who had proved his link to the gods. Oedipus kills a creature capable of sympathizing with him. Sophocles' audience must be aware of this irony. The Sphinx slayer discovers that his crime makes him a fellow of both his victims, Laius and the Sphinx. In slaying his father, inadvertently, Oedipus has become an actor in a cosmology, repeating the crime of Cronos and Zeus. Oedipus, sleeping with his mother, restages the primal incest of Uranus. This is the play within the play and the reason, perhaps, that the Greek audience accepted the exaggerated reactions of Jocasta and Oedipus, their willingness to abuse themselves as public spectacles. The mother is acting when she hangs herself, the son, acting when he blinds himself.

The agony of Sophocles' *Oedipus* is whether to believe in the justice and the truth of the gods. The notion of man as a possible demigod and a sharer in the mystery of divine incest, however, is never far from the play. Oedipus is a rival of the gods as a member of the royal family of Thebes, for the progenitor of Thebian kings, Cadmus, mated with a goddess, Harmonea, daughter of Ares the son of Zeus and Aphrodite. The goddess of love, Aphrodite, sprung from the white foam of Uranus's genitals, Zeus's grandfather. In sleeping with the daughter of Cadmus, Semele, Zeus is impregnating his great-granddaughter and his grandfather's great-granddaughter. (This is the union that Dionysus, who is half mortal, issues from.) Polydorus, the great-grandfather of Oedipus is half divine, a son of Cadmus and Harmonea, uncle of Dionysus. The reigning myth of Greek society, its cosmological explanation, was the ingestion of a son (Zeus) by a father (Cronus), the castration of a father (Uranus) by a son (Cronus), and a constant series of incestuous unions. It was religious myth, and its dramatization, although bent by Sophocles to the situation of the fifth century B.C.E., a religious crisis, needed no explanation.

It was quite different for Shakespeare, who stood on the brink of the modern age. The agony of Faust, of a man who may lose his soul, is part of Prince Hamlet's consciousness. It is, however, only one among a "Sea of troubles," as the threat of a father, the incest of a mother, and the question of private belief and right to enforce justice fight for attention in his "distracted" soul. The basis of Shakespeare's drama is his own intense, private life. It is personal. He does not have heroes: not Hamlet on the misty heights of Elsinore, or Lear in the shadows of druidic Britain, or Macbeth girdled by witches, whose genealogy can be traced back to the world of a credible myth. (Dante does this through the back door, by entering the world of myth directly and personally, but this could not be sustained on a public stage, nor attempted without the wings of Neoplatonic fantasy.[3]) Sophocles had just such a hero in Oedipus, and so did the other Greek tragedians drawing on figures like Orestes, Clytemnestra, and others. Shakespeare's intuition was to draw upon himself, his nightmares, to fill out these portraits and to give his drama that sense of the sacred and forbidden that would make them overwhelming on the stage. Shakespeare's taboos by necessity are personal.

If Shakespeare seems to many "absent," it is only because the playwright is in fact so "present." His tragic heroes fret with such uncanny life, drawn from the starts of his fantasies, as to completely fool the audience.

This was obscured because Shakespeare created not just characters as individuals but as "types," whose fate expressed some of the dilemmas of man as he moved into the secular modern world. Sophocles in the Oedipus cycle had done something similar for Greek society caught between the archaic age's acceptance of irresponsible brutal gods and the classical period's demand for justice or *dike,* right. Since there are so many types in Shakespeare, and all of his major work survives, his work has achieved the status of a religious literature. Hesiod and Homer took from a preexisting mythology, however, while Shakespeare could not borrow directly from a religious mythology that belonged to the church. Therefore he turned to history, folklore, chronicle, and to himself. Shakespeare is much more personal than Sophocles because he has to be if he is to find his riddles. It is this personal Shakespeare I am in search of.

Certainly I am not the first. There were Coleridge, Hazlitt, and then Borges, who wished to be "absent," a figment in the head of the Unknown. One of my favorite "searchers" is James Joyce. He has his tongue in his cheek. He has to be a bit "cute," given the Irish environment of *Ulysses.* So some of the remarks about Shakespeare in the National Library are obviously pedantic or sophomoric, borrowing from the atmosphere of slightly conceited prigs, in which Dedalus is speaking. With a startling insight, however, that his final disclaimer can not beg off, Joyce through Dedalus develops the idea of Anne Hathaway overmastering the young poet sexually and points to a series of references in the plays. "This is not altogether fool my Lord," as Kent points out to Lear in the Quarto, hearing the latter's jester jibe at reality. It is also Stephen's story, a story that never happens, the assignation with Molly Bloom. In that sense Joyce tells *his* story through the persona of Shakespeare, his own obsession with his wife. Joyce hears in Shakespeare, not absence, but presence.

Again the personal is obscured in Shakespeare because of the playwright's uncanny sense of sympathy. This endows major characters with a consciousness in which they are constantly examining their motives and calling their own actions into question. In *King Lear* we can easily see Cronus who cannibilizes his children, but we see something more, the anguish of Cronus before his children.

What strikes me as I read the plays over is not only the terror of the children before the father, as in *Hamlet* and *Lear* but the fear of the father, the anguish in being a father. This is particularly true of the two later plays, *Macbeth* and *The Tempest* where his own approaching old age is troubling Shakespeare.

As a writer of fiction, I could not help noticing a moment in *Hamlet* in which Shakespeare suddenly allows his prince—wrestling with the precepts of the church of Jesus, sin, salvation, the revenge of the other world—a direct link with the language of that strange gospel of Matthew, which I read as a late Jewish messianic text, a self-conscious deliberate reinterpretation of biblical lines to create a dramatic new Sampson. Matthew is a gospel of both belief and doubt, a doubt never successfully resolved in my, admittedly, skeptical reading. I noted with surprise, returning to *Hamlet*, after preparing a lecture on Matthew, that Hamlet's use of Matthew's expression about providence in the fall of a sparrow signals Shakespeare's very conscious embodiment in Hamlet of Jesus. Having said that, one is bound to draw conclusions. The moment in which Hamlet speaks as Jesus is not a moment of faith so much as the deepest disquiet: "how ill all's here about my heart," Jesus the night before the crucifixion, Jesus asking that the cup might pass from him, Jesus feeling terror before his fate, accepting it only because it is the will of the Father. The sense of the Father as being willing to sacrifice the Son on the altar of revenge is grim. It recalls an old West Semitic or Canaanite practice.[4] The fact that Shakespeare, through Hamlet, identifies, at this late moment in the play (when the Ghost has disappeared), with a son, willingly accepting the death ordained for him by a father, speaks to what a grim if angelic sense Shakespeare has of Hamlet's role. Shakespeare stands revealed before his audience between a dead father, his own, and a dead son, Hamnet, his own, in grief for a revenge that is beyond the power of man, but lies in the hands of darkness.

* * *

I stand at this far point from my first essay, which began as a few paragraphs on *Hamlet* in a letter to Cynthia Ozick from a cafe table in Buenos Aires. I realize looking back that I did not attempt the autobiographical riddle, although I was tempted to do so when I began. My own father had died, and I felt that the world was turned upside down. I was in a city staring at my familiar world, North America, from a global and perspective, upside down. (Argentina had just invaded the Malvinas/Falklands, which had turned Buenos Aires politically upside down. This also drew me to *Hamlet*, as political riddle.) Yes, I have spoken of Shakespeare and the father and son in the play, but to Shakespeare's father and son, what few shreds of fact we have about them, I have said nothing. Let me venture a guess, in the voice of that circular master,

Borges, down whose circular staircase in Buenos Aires I was once flung, to his cry: "I am old. I am blind. I have to earn my bread."(He had forgotten an earlier, importunate invitation for me to come at that hour and scheduled a working session with his translator.)

The shift from male to female, and the reversal of female into male and yet again, a turn, which is characteristic of the play *Macbeth* and its leading actor and actress, and the romance of the conch, descent to the sea floor, bestial and spiritual in the windings of the *Tempest*, suggest such a play of opposites, reversals, fathers and sons, in the puzzle of *Hamlet*. Why did Shakespeare settle on this old play, old plot, and give it such a brilliant turn, exactly when he did? Thoreau, another master of the sublimated has remarked on the necessity of poetry to be "written exactly at the right crisis," and a few sentences on: "It is only by a miracle that poetry is written at all. It is not recoverable thought, but a hue caught from a vaster receding thought." This speaks both to the moment in which Shakespeare wrote *Hamlet* and the sense of a glacial mass floating underneath the brilliant projection of the play upon the stage. The playwright's son and father had died. What guilt came upon Shakespeare's hands? The "death of Fathers," as Claudius remarks, seeming as sententious as his adviser Polonius, is a "common Theme," but it is not a "common Theme" when wound round with the death of sons. The guilt of a child descended from the country gentry and the rising bourgeoisie, fleeing his town, responsibilities, to write, to dream, in facing the all-powerful father, turns to a double haunting when he must face the ghost of the son as well. Must he pay for some disobedience to the father with the death of his own child? This is the story of Abraham and Terah, abandoned by the road in Haran and Isaac who must pay the penalty of Abraham on the slope of Mount Moriah. The terror of children expressed by Lady Macbeth, echoed in King Lear, and even still in *The Tempest*, is a far off echo of the crisis in which *Hamlet* was written.

It was a chance for the playwright to set himself in the howling wind of his own circular descent, the winding sheet of guilt and fear before death.

Notes

Chapter 1. The Absent Shakespeare

1. Jorge Luis Borges, "Everything and Nothing," in his *Labyrinths*, trans. James E. Irby (New York: New Directions Paperback, 1964), pp. 248–49.

2. These dates are given by Oscar James Campbell and Edward G. Quinn in *The Reader's Encyclopedia of Shakespeare* (New York: Crowell, 1966), pp. 284 and 428. Was Hamlet written in the consciousness of his father's death or dying? The tradition that Shakespeare himself played the ghost suggests both his identity and anger at the "dead father." Whereas in *Hamlet*, Shakespeare is wrestling with a son's anger and love for a scarce departed father, in *Lear*, the buried issue seems to me clearly a father's forbidden feelings for his children. Since Shakespeare's only son, Hamnet, had been dead since 11 August 1596, his two daughters, Susanna and Judith (and perhaps an ideal daughter created in the image of the dead Hamnet), had to be the nearest objects of his speculation. But more than any specific biographical inferences, it is the question of "the father" that gives these plays their magnetic attraction to each other, not who that father is.

3. Is that uniqueness stamped in each of us and each moment of time? The Greek conundrum of uniqueness or repetition in the space of the universe is still to be solved.

4. William Shakespeare, *The Parallel King Lear*, prepared by Michael Warren (Berkeley: University of California Press, 1989), the First Folio of 1623, afterwards, *FF*.4.1: 2221–22. All references hereafter to *King Lear* will be from this edition, which prints the First Folio of 1623 (hereafter *FF*.) on pages facing the The First Quarto of 1608 (hereafter *Q*.). The quarto version of this, although possibly a mistake, is quite funny: "As flies aretoth'wanton boyes, are we to th'Gods, / They bitt us for their sport" (*Q*.1952–53). The notion of boys "biting flies" is bizarre, rather the opposite is implied. (See my remarks in the chapter to follow on Steven Urkowitz's *Shakespeare's Revision of King Lear* in which the Folio is treated as Shakespeare's revision of the Quarto. The Folio shows throughout a more austere style, eschewing comic effects.) If this sense of man as a fly were Shakespeare's sentiment or even his King's, it would mean that only bleak cynicism, or actual nihilism, was at the center of the play. It is, however, a minor character, Gloucester, speaking. Failure to understand this leads Mary McCarthy into the error of attributing the words "Ripeness is all" (*FF*. 5.2: 2935) to King Lear as profound insight (Mary McCarthy, *Occasional Prose* [Harcourt Brace, 1985], p. 32). They are rather the trite catchwords of Edgar to his blind father, meant only to buck the stumbling graybeard up for the moment. Gloucester's dry reply in the Folio, missing from the Quarto, hardly assents to but rather mocks the overarching cliché, "And that's true too" (*FF*.5.2: 2936).

5. William Shakespeare, *Macbeth*, ed. Louis B. Wright and Virginia A. LaMar (New York: Pocket Books, The Folger Library Shakespeare, 1959).

6. A colleague, who was kind enough to review this text, sagely adds the

caution of Claudius, "Madness in great Ones, must not unwatch'd go" (F.F.3.1: 1846).

7. See Steven Urkowitz, *Shakespeare's Revision of King Lear* (Princeton: Princeton University Press, 1980), p. 3. "The Folio text represents a careful and dramatically sensitive revision of the Quarto; and . . . the revision could have been made by no one other than Shakespeare himself." As to the origin of the folio text, see Urkowitz, p. 13: "The Folio is a generally accurate reproduction of a promptbook which at some time regulated performance in the Globe playhouse." On the dangers in using a conflated text combining readings from both Quarto and Folio, see Urkowitz's remark concerning the changes to Kent's lines about the French invasion from Quarto to Folio:

> Instead of providing a "good" text for readers, actors, and literary scholars, modern editors accidently disguise the integrity of the two early versions of this passage. Although editors often mark with brackets the lines unique to the Quarto, these warnings have never been understood. During the past thirty years not one literary or dramatic analysis of this scene makes any reference to the original texts. . . . For the major variants in the Folio version of *King Lear*, only one explanation does not require the acceptance of hypotheses that are either demonstrably false or so complex as to be patently improbable. The explanation is that the Quarto was printed from Shakespeare's foul papers, and the Folio was printed from the Quarto version that was carefully brought into agreement with the official promptbook. The promptbook itself embodied all of Shakespeare's own revisions, including additions, cuts, substitutions and rearrangements. The Quarto and Folio do not represent two partial copies of a single original, but instead they are different stages of a composition, an early and a final draft. Except for only a very few variants that are obviously the result of errors in copying or printing, the vast majority of the changes found in the Folio must be accepted as Shakespeare's final decisions. The modern practice of printing a composite text eclectically chosen from the Quarto and Folio seriously distorts Shakespeare's most profound play (Urkowitz, *Shakespeare's Revision*, p. 79 and 129).

Chapter 2. All the King's Daughters

1. Urkowitz, *Shakespeare's Revision*, p. 100.

2. This mutes the political disaster, further lending credence to Steven Urkowitz's thesis in *Shakespeare's Revision* about Albany's loss of political rationale. If there are "Spies and Speculations / Intelligent of our State" (F.F.2.4: 1633–34) within the English camp to France and Cordelia, as Kent avers, the notion of English loyalty to the Dukes is cast into doubt.

3. See Eric Partridge, *Shakespeare's Bawdy* (New York: Dutton, 1960), p. 106. "Eel is erotic-suggestive of penis in 'Thunder shall not so awake the beds of eels as my giving out her beauty stir up the lewdly inclined,' *Pericles*, 4,2,144–146; cf. the *double entente* of the erotically minded: *a snake in the grass* (a penis amid its circumambient hair.)" Coxcomb, obviously also suggests the erotic. See also Partridge, *Shakespeare's Bawdy*, p. 88: "cock. Penis . . . . L. *coccus*, the male domestic fowl: probably echoic of its cry (cf. **cuckoo**). Hence applied to 'objects supposed to represent cock's head and comb: *watercock &c.*', especially cock (short for *watercock*) and tap: hence, *cock* = 'penis,' not only from the shape but also from the fact that the penis emits water (as does a tap) and sperm." The image of the live eels trying to jump up from the paste while the cockney—notice how the obscene word cock is suggested both in cockney and coxcomb—raps them on their red flaring heads has a double force. On the one hand anger is being forced

down; on the other, the cock is being forced back into the medium of the paste, which suggests sexual intercourse. So the final cry "down, wantons, down" suggests that the phallus or eel is being knocked back from its assault on the cook as it comes up, but it can also imply that it is being pushed down into the vagina. Both the ambiguity of up and down in lovemaking and that of Lear's love and hate seem to me implicit.

4. See Partridge, *Shakespeare's Bawdy*, p. 165: "**Pillicock; Pillicock Hill.** Lear's 'Twas this flesh begot Those pelican daughters' prompts Edgar (outcast and posing as idiot Poor Tom) to chant, 'Pillicock sat on Pillicock Hill' . . . . The usual *langue-verte* explanation is that Pillicock (penis [cf. pin] + cock = penis, and that *Pillicock-hill* = pudend; but more probably *Pillicock* = male generative organs (*pill*, 'testicle'; [i.e.,] euphony-convenient; *cock*, 'penis') and *Pillicock-hill* = the mount of Venus + the *pudendum muliebre* itself. It is a common error, even among the less 'innocent' of Shakespeare's commentators, to oversimplify his subtle sexuality." The Quarto gives another version of the cry that follows the reference to Pillicock Hill, "a lo lo lo" (Q.3.4: 1597). One editor transcribes "Haloo, haloo, loo, loo." This, like Kittredge's suggestion cited in the Arden Shakespeare, p. 112: "A wild 'haloo' as if he were calling a hawk," or Craig's "A cry to excite dogs," seems wide of the mark. Curling the tongue back in the throat—pushing it forward, trilling in ululating falsetto "alowlowlooloo" while bouncing up and down as if in copulation, Edgar simulates sexual bliss, becoming man in the act of the "bare, forked Animal" as Lear observes. If the first syllables are pronounced "allow, allow," an eerie subliminal message of permission seems to escape Poor Tom's lips to the King.

5. This direction by indirection is one of the unique characteristics of Shakespeare's poetry and stagecraft. Ophelia, also in the guise of a madwoman, will speak truth.

6. Both Lear and Gloucester seem to die of heart attacks. "Pray you undo this Button . . ." (*FF*.5.3: 3281), three lines before his last, indicates some sort of seizure, which is seen in the actor as a sudden difficulty in breathing.

7. This may imply an attempt to revive Cordelia by King Lear, bending to shake her awake, coax, ask her during the series, "Never?" The five "nevers" are hammer strokes to the nihilism, the "nothing," which is the drama's refrain.

Chapter 3. The Itch Revises

1. See William Shakespeare, *Hamlet*, The Arden Shakespeare, ed. Harold Jenkins (London: Routledge, 1990), p. 295, n. 119. For a more detailed discussion of the sexual connotations of "nothing" in *Hamlet* refer to pp. 77–78.

2. The force of interruptions in *King Lear* is detailed in Urkowitz, *Shakespeare's Revision*.

> The straightforward dramatic use of the rhetorical figure aposiopesis, a sudden breaking off of a sentence for emotional emphasis, exemplifies a device that is sometimes perfectly consonant with non-dramatic usages.

> I will have such revenges on you both,
> That all the world shall—I will do such things,
> What they are yet, I know not, but they shalbe
> The terrors of the earth?

(Folio, 1579–82; 2.4.279–82)

In a monologue or within a long speech the interruption of a regular grammatical pattern signals that the speaker is in the throes of some passion. The device calls attention to the internal state of the speaker. However, if a speech is broken off in the course of a dialogue a different effect is achieved. The interruption then indicates a state of tension existing in a relationship. Such an interrupted speech points to a dramatic situation *between* characters (p. 18).

The consequences of these interruptions, not only of individual speeches, but also of exits and formal patterns are detailed by Urkowitz (pp. 63–67). The audience is frustrated at the very moment when it has been led to expect the "peaceful reconciliation" of Gloucester and Edgar, Lear and Cordelia. It dramatizes and makes the audience share in what Shakespeare is struggling with—the impossibility of reconciliation between daughter and father, father and son.

3. This is emphasized in the Folio, a few lines on, by the addition of "fine word: Legitimate" (*FF.*1.2: 352) as Edmund boasts of his verbal acumen to the audience.

4. Note that Edmund, in the Folio, is the one who first mentions *Tom* o'Bedlam and plays at being *Tom* o'Bedlam, sighing in an insane manner. It is Edmund who unwittingly suggests to Edgar, the disguise by which the latter will preserve his life.

5.   When we our betters see bearing our woes: we scarcely
     think, our miseries, our foes.
     Who alone suffers suffers, most it'h mind,
     Leaving free things and happy shows behind,
     But then the mind much sufferance doth or'e skip,
     When grief hath mates, and bearing fellowship:
     How light and portable my pain seems now,
     When that which makes me bend, makes the King bow.
     He childed as I fathered, *Tom* away,
     Mark the high noises and thy self bewray.
     When false opinion whose wrong thoughts defile thee,
     In thy just proof repeals and reconciles thee,
     What will hap more to night, safe scape the King,
     Lurk, lurk.

                               (*Q.*3.6: 1793–1806)

Chapter 4. Hamlet's Father

1. In fact, if *Hamlet*, *King Lear*, and *The Tempest*, the three plays that seem to bear on Shakespeare's dream life, are subtracted from the corpus of his dramatic work, a great playwright, but not the Shakespeare we know, would exist in English literature—one whose genius was comedy and whose tragedies would seem to be written on narrow and explicit themes: jealousy, ambition (*Othello*, *Macbeth*). A quiet, detached pessimism would be the sounding board then of Shakespeare at his most profound, a kind of autumn wisdom, with its furthest reach in the dark comedies. Then indeed one might agree with Borges and see him as a master of masks who never chose to reveal himself but only his sensibility in his dramatic creation.

2. Harry Levin, *The Question of Hamlet* (New York: Oxford University Press, 1978), p. 49. I have used the Folio citation of the lines "The Funeral bakt-meats" rather than Professor Levin's in order to remain consistent.

3. Act 3, scene 2 is the natural place for the revenge to take place, in front of

the assembled court as the play "catches" Claudius's conscience. Hamlet has cast himself, however, not as actor in this drama, but director and playwright of it. He forgets the role the Ghost has assigned him so far as to cry out in triumph at the performance, "Would not this Sir, and a Forest of Feathers, if the rest of / my Fortunes turn Turk with me; with two Provincial / Roses on my rac'd Shoes, get me a Fellowhip in a cry / of Players sir" (*FF*.3.2: 2147–50). His very role here precludes revenge, and, when he has recovered himself and is ready to "drink hot blood," Claudius too has changed roles. I am not talking about Hamlet's dilemma in getting free of the courtiers and the false friends, Guildenstern and Rosencrantz, or of separating Claudius from the Queen, his prayers, etc., but rather Shakespeare's determination to deny the Prince his opportunity.

4. See T. S. Eliot, "Hamlet and His Problems," in *Twentieth Century Interpretations of Hamlet* (Englewood Cliffs, N.J.: Prentice Hall, 1968), pp. 25–26.

5. What if it tempt you toward the Flood my Lord?
   Or to the dreadful Sonnet of the Cliff,
   That beetles o're his base into the Sea,
   And there assumes some other horrible form,
   which might deprive your Sovereignty of Reason
   And draw you into madness think of it?

   (*FF*.1.4: 658–63)

Here the Folio ends, but the Quarto goes on. It seems that Horatio suspects the Ghost, does not see it as benign, but has a strong sense that it is a malignant "form" tempting the Prince to his death.

The very place puts toys of desperation
Without more motive, into every brain
That looks so man fathoms to the sea
And hears it roar beneath.

(Q2.D2.1.4.75–78)

6. Quarto and Folio differ on this line. On the page, the Quarto version seems more lucid: "thou would'st not / think how ill all's here about my heart, but it is no matter" (*Q*.N3v.5.2.201–202), as against the Folio's: "but thou wouldest not think how all here a- / bout my heart: but it is no matter." The Folio, however, leaves unsaid what is about Hamlet's heart, and it may be that the actor's pause here, and breaking off, to remark, "but it is no matter," is more "pregnant." (Subsequent to writing this, I discovered in Steven Urkowitz's, "Burying Three Hamlets," in *Shakespeare Study Today*, ed. Georgianna Ziegler [New York: AMS Press, 1986], pp. 55–57, an almost identical reading of this line.)

7. It has been objected that the "questionable shape" refers to the ghost's armor, his "complete steel," and to the reason for being up in arms so. Yet this question is posed specifically a few moments later:

What may this mean?
That thou dead Corse again in complete steel,
Revisits thus the glimpses of the Moon,
Making Night hideous . . . ?

(*FF*.1.4: 636–39)

The expression "questionable shape" on the other hand comes earlier and at the end of lines that *question* not the appearance of the ghost in armor but its intent, "charitable" or "wicked." Something about the shape of the apparition is disquieting, "questionable." Even the lines that directly follow show this apprehension, reserve, on the part of the Prince. He does not directly call out, "*Hamlet*, / King, Father, Royal Dane" to the shade. He deliberately sets up distance, a question, by declaring, "I'll call thee *Hamlet*, / King, Father, Royal Dane" (*FF*.1.4: 629–30).

8. Note that in the Folio, as opposed to the Second Quarto, the Ghost here calls his son by name. "List Hamlet, oh list, / If thou didst ever thy dear Father love." The line in *Q2.D2*ᵛ is, "list, list, o list: / If thou did'st ever thy dear father love." It is a slight touch, but it deepens the horror in this exchange of personal names between them.

9. As Professor Edward Quinn, pointed out to me, Hamlet does not in a straightforward fashion ever call the Ghost, "Father." "Thou com'st in such a questionable shape / That I will speake to thee. Ile call thee *Hamlet*, / King, Father, Royal Dane: Oh, oh, answer me . . ." (*FF*.1.4: 628–30). This is a very qualified "Father." For Hamlet only *proposes* to call the Ghost "Father," though the actor may inflect this series of names so as to actually call them out over the battlements, hoping to awaken an affectionate or authoritative response.

10. I have used in this instance, the Quarto's "sullied" rather than "solid." The possibility that Shakespeare indeed meant "sallied" in the Quarto, as if the sallies of Gertrude and Claudius were abusing him, can not be excluded either. This is one of the words that bedevil the editors of conflated editions. See for instance the remarks of Edward Hubler, the Signet edition's editor, who gives the following explanation for choosing "sullied." "Q2 has *sallied*, here modernized to *sullied*, which makes sense and is therefore given; but the Folio reading, *solid*, which fits better with *melt*, is quite possibly correct"; William Shakespeare, *Hamlet*, ed. Edward Hubler (New York: NAL, Signet, 1963), p. 44.

11. It is true that Hamlet, in act 3, scene 2, answers Rosencrantz's query, "what is your cause of distem- / per?" with the blunt, "Sir I lack Advancement." Further, to Rosencrantz's protest that he has the voice of the King for his succession to the throne of Denmark, Hamlet observes wryly, "I, but while the grass grows, the Proverb is / something musty." But it is not clear whether Hamlet is simply dissimulating here to keep the two false friends off the track of his revenge. When the Prince speaks to Horatio here, the audience understands that from the beginning (quite apart from his uncle's marriage to Gertrude and the subsequent disclosure of treachery), Hamlet has been angered by Claudius's succession to a throne which the Prince expected.

12. Ernest Jones, *Hamlet and Oedipus* (Garden City, N.Y.: Anchor Books, 1954), p. 18.

13. S. T. Coleridge, from the Lectures of 1811–12, Lecture 12, *Shakespearian Criticism*, edited by Thomas Middleton Raysor (New York: Dutton, 1960). Reprinted in *Hamlet*, edited by Edward Hubler (New York: Signet, 1963), p. 192.

14. The Folio's cuts are instructive. Claudius's false compassion, "Alas, alas," is out of place here, and the riddle of the worm eating the body of a dead king, emerging as bait for a living fish, which suggests that Hamlet has knowledge of his father's murder, is perhaps too arcane for the audience. Hamlet's "fat King, / and your lean Beggar," prepares the insult to Claudius's pretension of royalty well enough.

15. As noted previously, "old Mole" expresses more than the humor of Hamlet's anxiety before the Ghost. It indicates fear and perhaps hostility.

16. One may say that some urging of "conscience" drives Ophelia to suicide. But Hamlet has defined for us that it is exactly "Conscience" that makes, "Cow-

ards of us all" (3.1: 1737), restraining us from coming to death by our own hand. He may mock his "Conscience" in this regard, even resent it, but he ultimately respects its claims. Ophelia obviously does not if she can be held culpable in her own death. To the latter question, however, like the "questionable shape" of the Ghost, Shakespeare will not give a clear answer. The description of her floating in a bed of flowers, being dragged down by the weight of the water in her skirts suggests insanity. Yet the gravediggers mock the official account, the finding of the inquest that her drowning was not willful. The priest pronounces that "her death was doubtful." Indeed everything about Ophelia is "doubtful": whether she really loves Hamlet, whether she is a willing spy for her father, whether she recognizes at the end the evil of Claudius. It is an inspired joke that Hamlet should send her a poem of doubts:

> Doubt thou, the Stars are fire,
> Doubt, that the Sun doth move:
> Doubt Truth to be a Liar,
> But never Doubt, I love.

(FF.2.2: 1144–47)

17. After the fact, he cries "I took thee for thy Betters" (FF.3.4: 2414). This is hardly an acceptable excuse for not drawing the curtain in a court full of informers. It is especially "questionable" given the moral punctiliousness just shown by Hamlet on the stairs before the kneeling Claudius.

18. A colleague has objected that this may not mean suicide but only "everyday pleasure." Clearly, however, the dramatic context points to suicide. Horatio has just offered to drink the poison that is left in the cup: "I am more an Antique Roman than a Dane. / Here's yet some Liquor left" (FF.5.2: 3826–27). Hamlet grabs his hand; "As th'art a man, give me the Cup. / Let go. By Heaven, I'll have't" (FF.5.2: 3828–29). Given these stage directions indicated in the lines, a tussle over the cup of poison, one must read "Absent thee from felicity awhile," followed as in the next line by, "And in this harsh world draw thy breath in pain," as a mordant joke about the joy of suicide or passing (as Hamlet is doing) into the other world.

19. Spelled "Akers" in the Folio, which may suggest a pun on ache, recalling the line earlier in the scene, "Did these bones cost no more the breeding, but / to play at Loggets with 'em? mine ake to think / on't" (FF.5.1: 3281–83).

20. Maynard Mack remarks on this in "The World of Hamlet," Yale Review 41 (1952): 502–23. "In the last act of the play (or so it seems to me, for I know there can be differences on this point), Hamlet accepts his world and we discover a different man. Shakespeare does not outline for us the process of acceptance any more than he had done with Romeo or was to do with Othello. But he leads us strongly to expect an altered Hamlet, and then, in my opinion, provides him. We must recall that at this point Hamlet has been absent from the stage during several scenes and that such absences in Shakespearian tragedy usually warn us to be on the watch for a new phase in the development of the character. . . . Hamlet now looks different. He is wearing a different dress—probably, as Granville-Barker thinks, his 'seagown scarf'd' about him, but in any case no longer the disordered costume of his antic disposition. The effect is not entirely dissimilar to that in Lear, when the old king wakes out of his madness to find fresh garments on him." Mack speaks of the graveyard scene but in general terms: "The crucial evidence of Hamlet's new frame of mind, as I understand it, is the graveyard

scene. Here, in its ultimate symbol, he confronts, recognizes, and accepts the condition of being man."

21. The prediction is Claudius's (*FF*.3.1: 1828–32), speaking to Polonius. It is not clear at this point, before Hamlet's direct affront to Claudius at the performance of *The Mousetrap* whether the latter is preparing to have Hamlet murdered in England. Polonius suggests the subterfuge of using Gertrude to try and discover Hamlet's thoughts before either confining him or sending him to England. There is a curious parallel between this speech and the first one of Claudius to Hamlet, for in both, although the speaker is not aware of it, there is wisdom even in the hypocrisy of the good wishes. This of course is the mark of the poisoner, evil concealed in a bouquet.

Chapter 5. The Shadow's Dance

1. In the following discussion, it would be well to keep in mind the distinctions drawn between the editions of the Quarto by Steven Urkowitz in his essay, "Burying Three Hamlets," pp. 45–46: "*Hamlet* was first printed in a 1603 Quarto; then it was 'Newly imprinted and enlarged to almost as much againe as it was, according to the true and perfect Coppie' in a Second Quarto dated 1605; and finally it appearred in an another altered form, 'Published according to the True Originall Copies' in the 1623 First Folio . . . . Although the conventional or current orthodox explanation of the First Quarto holds that 'pirates' produced its variations from the 'true Shakespearian text,' this explanation skips over consideration of consistent patterns of variation and large, coherent structural changes. If the differences between Q1 and Q2 indeed result from 'pirates' we'll see that these pirates should merit further study, for their theatrical acuity is impressive. And if actors' errors were responsible for variants between Q2 and the Folio text, then we should certainly study their patterns of blunder, since they seem to resemble those of another actor we are very interested in, one William Shakespeare."

2. The speech was first taken out of context, the film script beginning with the lines, "So oft it chances in particular men . . . ." and ending with "take corruption / From that particular fault." The director could not forego adding some crude ones of his own, which only point out how wide he was of Shakespeare's intentions, i.e., "This is the tragedy of a man who could not make up his mind." The speech is then, repeated where it occurs in the Quarto, act 1, scene 4.

3. Reference to the First or "Bad" Quarto of 1603 indicates that a fragment of this line was originally in the acting text, was deleted in a subsequent version, the Second Quarto, and then restored in the Folio. The First Quarto is so crude in many parts that it is hard to accept it as Shakespeare's first version of *Hamlet* especially as the Second Quarto whose publication followed it by only a year or two is such a fuller and more mature version of the play, showing very little of the jingling and blatant stage indicators that afflict the Quarto of 1603. This, however, is an unresolved question. The Quarto of 1603 may well be a corrupt, unauthorized, version of *Hamlet* in certain passages. The omission, however, in the Second Quarto of a line that will reappear in the Folio, points to the strong possibility of the First Quarto reflecting a draft of *Hamlet* that is earlier than the Second Quarto's, a line that Shakespeare cut from his second draft and then restored to his third. As Steven Urkowitz has demonstrated in his remarks on Gertrude and Laertes, which I quote further on, the changes between First and Second Quarto

reflect much more than line readings; they indicate very different ideas of whom these characters are. If Shakespeare was experimenting, much like a modern playwright during pre-Broadway tryouts, with the audience's reaction to this play, such changes would not be surprising. The sexually charged scene between Ophelia and Hamlet in the First Quarto at the dumb show is also characterized by the use of the word "poopies" for breasts, the allusion to puppets being understood, and the misinterpretation about where Hamlet should put his head.

> *Ham.* . . . Lady will you give me leave, and so forth:
> To lay my head in your lap?
> *Ofel.* No my Lord.
> *Ham.* Upon your lap, what do you think I meant contrary matters?
> [*Enter in a Dumb Show, the King and the Queen* . . .]
>
>   (Q1.F3: 3.2)

Whether the First Quarto's ambiguous "and so forth" refers to a stage gesture of the hands, or an ironic reference to politeness, as Hamlet motions an intention to dive between Ophelia's legs, is not clear. Something of the latter nature, however, is suggested by his clarification, "Upon your lap." The Second Quarto cut the misunderstanding away, but added, "That's a fair thought to lie between Maids legs." The Folio, restored the misunderstanding, "Lady, shall I lye in your Lap?" Hamlet asks. To which, Ophelia responds, "No." After Hamlet's clarification, "I mean, my Head upon your Lap?" however, she grants permission, "I my Lord." Whatever the stage business was, it worked better with the misunderstanding about the lap and its pointed reference to fornication and perhaps cunnilingus. Shakespeare in the Folio, wishing to strengthen Ophelia and Hamlet's sexual play on stage, restored and refurbished the lines of the First Quarto, kept the additions of the Second, and gave this byplay further lines as well.

4. Harold Jenkins, in Shakespeare, *Hamlet* (Arden), p. 295, nn. 115 and 119.

5. Again the First Quarto seems to clarify the stage business. There a puppet show was clearly indicated, which Hamlet offered to interpret, but the Prince referred directly to Ophelia's breasts or buttocks as the "poopies" at which he was staring. In the Second Quarto and the Folio, this coarseness is softened by the inversion of the imagery. The stage business remains the same, probably a look into her bosom or motion toward her backside, but the language is reversed, as Hamlet refers to Ophelia's "poopies" or "puppets." ("Poop" is used elsewhere in Shakespeare's works with sexual connotations, to refer to the hindquarters or buttocks, as in *Anthony and Cleopatra*, or a verb as in, Pericles 4.2.23–24: "Ay she quickly poopt him; she made him roast-meat for worms." See *Partridge, Shakespeare's Bawdy*, p. 169: "To infect with venereal disease."

6. The following passage from Q2 and Folio, illustrate the latter's condensation.

> But woe is me, you are so sick of late,
> So far from cheer, and from our former state,
> That I distrust you, yet though I distrust,
> Discomfort you my Lord it nothing must.
> For women fear too much, even as they love,
> And womens fear and love hold quantity,
> Either none, in neither ought, or in extremity,
> Now what my Lord is proof hath made you know,
> And as my love is siz'd, my fear is so,

Where love is great, the littlest doubts are fear,
Where little fears grow great, great love grows there.

(Q2.H^v–H2: 3.2.154–64)

But woe is me, you are so sick of late,
So far from cheer, and from your forme[r] state,
That I distrust you: yet though I distrust,
Discomfort you (my Lord) it nothing must:
For womens Fear and Love, holds quantity,
in neither ought, or in extremity:
Now what my love is, proof hath made you know,
And as my Love is siz'd, my fear is so.

(FF.3.2: 2032–39)

Nor earth to me give food, nor heaven light,
Sport and repose lock from me day and night,
To desperation turn my trust and hope,
And Anchors cheer in prison be my scope,
Each opposite that blanks the face of joy,
Meet what I would have well, and it destroy,
Both here and hence pursue me lasting strife,
If once I be a widow, ever I be a wife.

(Q2.H2^v: 3.2.208–15)

Nor Earth to me give food, nor Heaven light
Sport and repose lock from me day and night:
Each opposite that blanks the face of joy,
Meet what I would have well, and it destroy:
Both here, and hence, pursue me lasting strife,
If once a Widow, ever I be Wife.

(FF. 3.2: 2084–89)

7. The Folger Library edition explains, "better" to mean "wittier," and "worse" more offensive, also parodying the marriage service, "for better and worse" an allusion that Hamlet picks up and replies to with, "So you mistake Husbands" (Folio). (The Second Quarto reads, "So you mistake **your** husbands." The First Quarto reads "So you **must take** your husband.")

8. This comes many lines after the moment when Ophelia sings openly of her wish to give Hamlet her virginity. In the First Quarto these slightly salacious verses, "To morrow is saint Valentine's Day, / All in the morning betime, / And a maid at your window, / To be your Valentine: / The young man rose, and dan'd his clothes, / and dupt the chamber door, / Let in the maid, that out a maid, / Never departed more" (Q1. H2), follow lines about Ophelia's father's death when she enters the scene again to meet Laertes. In the Second Quarto and Folio, Shakespeare has Ophelia sing them earlier in the presence of Gertrude, Claudius, and Horatio. The playwright must have felt that the sexual innuendo was inappropriate with Laertes present. It is grief for her father Ophelia sings of to her brother, not of her intact virginity, frustrated (by her father) now forever. The mistake made in most productions is not to imagine Ophelia's madness in terms of Hamlet's, i.e., "I essentially am not in madness, / but mad in craft," as the latter admits to Gertrude. Medical practitioners and religious authorities must debate whether committing suicide is madness. Laertes does not reveal his "thoughts" to his sister as she asks him to. I don't think it farfetched to imagine that Ophelia is as angry at her father and brother as she is at Hamlet. Her pointed remark to

Gertrude, "Where is the beauteous Majesty of Denmark" (*FF.*4.5: 2767), indicates that Ophelia blames the Queen too for her behavior. Hamlet's murdering of Polonius has made his daughter's marriage almost hopeless., Laertes's murderous intentions now promise a final disaster. Who is to judge, except by "canon," that Ophelia's suicide is inappropriate?

It is exactly Ophelia's dilemma that explains her riddles. She is jumping between her erotic frustration at losing her lover and her grief in the wake of her father's death. Since thoughts of one bring up thoughts of the other, she has no refuge. Her father has driven away her lover, her lover has killed her father.

9. "They say the Owl was / a Bakers daughter. Lord, we know what we are, but / know not what we may be" (*FF.* 4.5: 2784–86). The riddles are so complex that Ophelia may not indeed deliver them as veiled innuendoes, but utter them in a manic state.

10. There are a number of small changes in the Folio following Hamlet's and Ophelia's exchange, generally improvements on the Second Quarto, in particular, Hamlet's line restored from the First Quarto: "What, frighted with false fire." (the First Quarto reads "fires"). This makes the cry for "Light" in the darkness of Claudius's conscience a moment later, more pointed. (Olivier in his movie *Hamlet* seized a torch here to look at Claudius's face in a whirling of lights, an apt staging of the dilemma).

11. Q2.I.3: 3.4.71 reads "iudgement."

12. In the Quarto, Hamlet enters talking to himself, then tells himself (or the audience) he hears Rosencranz coming, and, finally, rather awkwardly announces his pursuers entrance: "Safely stowed, but soft, what noise, who calls on **Hamlet**? / O here they come." (Q2.K^v: 4.2.1–4) The Folio breaks this up.

> *Enter Hamlet.*
> Ham. Safely stowed.
> *Gentlemen within. Hamlet,* Lord *Hamlet.*
> Ham. What noise? Who calls on *Hamlet?*
> Oh here they come. *Enter Ros. and Guildensterne.*

Steven Urkowitz, in *Shakespeare's Revision*, ch. 3, gives a convincing demonstration of the sophistication of the Folio over the Quarto exits and entrances in the putative revision of *King Lear*.

13. See *FF.* 3.4: 2570–72, Where Hamlet warns Gertrude, not to be "like the famous Ape / To try Conclusions in the Basket, creep / And break your own neck down." This is echoed by his warning to Rosencrantz and Guildenstern, that they are Claudius's sponges: "He keeps them like an Ape in / the corner of his jaw, first mouth'd to be last swallowed . . ." (*FF.* 4.1: 2647–48). The "apple" in the corner of the jaw of the Second Quarto, "such Officers do the King best service in the end, he / keeps them like an apple in the corner of his jaw . . . " confuses the image of the sponge and loses the ominous force of the repetition.

14. Urkowitz, "Burying Three *Hamlets*," pp. 46–48.

15. It is peculiar that Gertrude's speech in the Second Quarto apologizing at the grave side for Hamlet's outburst is transferred to the King in the Folio: "This is mere Madness: / And thus a while the fit will work on him: / Anon as patient as the female Dove, / When that her golden Couplet are disclos'd: / His silence will sit drooping" (*FF.* 5.1: 3482–86). It makes Claudius seem sympathetic to Hamlet. Is this part of the counterfeiting—an instance of Claudius's new found confidence in his treachery and his desire to forestall a collision between Laertes and Hamlet before the fencing match can achieve its aim? This would be the reflection

of a playwright who after many performances could seize the opportunity for a twist of irony. "Good *Gertrude*, set some watch over your Son" (*FF.* 5.1: 3495) signals that the King senses Gertrude watching his confidential whisper to Laertes. It completes the royal couple's alienation although Claudius seems unaware of the danger to him in this.

16. Urkowitz, "Burying Three Hamlets," p. 49.

17. Claudius is unconsciously speaking of his own condition. the audience has seen him trying to enact penitence and sorrow and failing after his start at the play Hamlet arranged. Prince Hamlet uses this imagery to Ophelia and to himself, speaking of the actor's face and emotions, holding up the portrait of his father to his mother, and talking of the replication of images, his father's and Claudius's, in popular esteem.

18. Among the Folio cuts is the omission of a redundancy and fixing of a preposition in the exchange of remarks about hot and cold: "But yet me thinks it is very sully [sultry] and hot, or my complexion" (Q2.N2: 5.2.98–99) as against the "Me thinks it is very sultry, and hot for my / Complexion."

19. There seems to be a missing comma after "knows"—the Signet edition places the comma there, rather than after "leaves" although the meaning could support two strong pauses, both after "leaves" and "knows."

20. That Claudius is forced back on such instruments to work his will, as in the case of Polonius, suggests how tenuous Hamlet's uncle's position is as king. During the rebellion led by Laertes, Claudius has no support at all in the court. The ambassadors he sends to Norway, Voltemand and Cornelius, are conspicuously absent. Claudius has to use Rosencrantz and Guildenstern for his dirty business.

Chapter 6. Macbeth's Child

1. Lily B. Campbell, "Macbeth: A Study in Fear," in her *Shakespeare's Tragic Heroes* (New York: Barnes and Noble, 1967), p. 208.

2. W. B. Yeats, "Crazy Jane Talks with The Bishop," in his *The Collected Poems* (New York: Macmillan, 1958), p. 254.

3. Stephen Booth notices this glaring omission of an heir although he comes to very different conclusions. "Lady Macbeth's mysteriously missing children present an ominous, unknown, but undeniable time before the beginning. Doubtful beginnings are also incidentally inherent in such details of the play as Macduff's non-birth. Indeed, the beginnings, sources, causes, of almost everything in the play are at best nebulous"; Stephen Booth, *King Lear, Macbeth, Indefinition, & Tragedy* (New Haven: Yale University Press, 1983), p. 94.

4. It is exactly in terms of the germination of seed that Banquo questions the witches, as if telling them in his phrasing what is on his mind, what he wants them to predict.

If you can look into the seeds of time
And say which grain will grow and which will not,
Speak then to me. . . .

(1.3.63–65)

The playwright's obsession with conception, seed, what will come to birth and what will not—the stillborn line and the fecund—are appropriate to Banquo, who is thinking of his line of descent and to whom this "greater happiness" will

be given. (Indeed there is some malice to Macbeth in the rhetoric of Banquo's "which will not.") Again it is Banquo, who sniffing the air of the castle, sees a very different set of birds than Lady Macbeth's cawing, carrion-seeking ravens. Banquo's summer guest "the temple-haunting martlet" who not only chirps there but also builds a "pendent bed," or nest, which that passive hoper after Duncan's throne describes, with irony perhaps, as a "procreant cradle" (1.6.9).

5. This may bear on one of the riddles of the play, deliberately posed several times but never answered—why Macduff leaves his wife and child behind. Malcolm can not understand how a father would leave a wife and child in the grip of Macbeth's power and revenge—he has good reason to suspect Macduff's intentions in appearing before him: "Why in that rawness left you wife and child, / Those precious motives, those strong knots of love, / Without leave-taking?" (4.3.30–32). Macduff gives no answer to this, but makes to break off abruptly his suit to Malcolm. Lady Macduff has been even more bitter just before her murder, addressing her son as "fatherless," speaking of the absent Macduff who has deserted them as "one that swears, and lies" teasing her "Poor prattler" who keeps insisting that his father still lives (4.2). Is it Macduff's willingness to sacrifice his child and heir for the sake of his country, Scotland, not the caul of his birth, that in truth armors him against Macbeth? Or is the act of leaving wife and children behind part of the grim riddle of manhood in the tragedy, that without the "milk" of pity, tears for his own child, Macduff can be called "none of woman born"?

6. It is significant that Macbeth is not confused by their bisexual appearance, but rather accepts it, perhaps as an image of his own confusion of nature, male and female.

7. The threat of the world of the dead to break out of its confinement and overwhelm the living is part of the terror of *Macbeth*. It is given tongue by Macbeth at the moment when Banquo's ghost appears: "If charnel houses and our graves must send / Those that we bury back, our monuments / Shall be the maws of kites. . . . The time has been / That, when the brains were out, the man would die, / And there's an end! But now they rise again. . . ." (3.4.87–89 and 96–98). From the very beginning of *Macbeth*, as I have argued, the dead son of Macbeth may be haunting his parents. This is linked to Horatio's speech in *Hamlet* where the world of the dead also threatens the living: "A little ere the mightiest *Julius* fell / The graves stood tenantless, and the sheeted dead / Did squeak and gibber in the Roman streets" (Q2.B.2ᵛ: 1.1.114–16). This in fact describes the grimmest anxiety of Prince Hamlet, whose father shadows him from the grave through half the play. It suggests that Shakespeare's dead child is casting the shadow of pathos through these two dramas.

8. See U. Cassuto, *A Commentary on the Book of Genesis*, Part One (Jerusalem: Magnes Press, 1972), pp. 21–24.

9. Alfred Harbage, "Introduction," in William Shakespeare, *Macbeth* (Baltimore: Penguin, 1956), pp. 16–17.

10. See, for instance, after the appearance of Banquo's ghost, Macbeth's question, "What is the night?" and Lady Macbeth's reply, "Almost at odds with morning, which is which" (3.4.157–58).

11. See for instance, "This is the very ecstasy of Love," (*Hamlet* FF.2.1: 999) and "allay thy ecstasy, / In measure rein thy joy." (*Merchant of Venice*, FF. 3.2: 1457–58).

12. See William Shakespeare, *Macbeth*, ed. Kenneth Muir (London: Routledge, The Arden Shakespeare, 1989), p. 38, n. 7: ". . . *jump*] i.e. risk. Cf. *Cym.*, v.iv. 188: 'Jump the after-enquiry at your own peril.' But it might perhaps mean 'skip over' or 'evade' (the thought of the life to come)." The attempt to juggle or "equivocate

to heaven" is echoed by the drunken Porter, as Muir points out citing Dowden, who suggested that it was "an unconscious reference to Macbeth." The idea of dramatizing the equivocation, implicit in Macbeth's process of thought as he wonders whether he should "jump the life to come" may derive from the reaction in 1606 against the priest, Garnet. Muir, in discussing the dating of *Macbeth*, cites the public furor over Father Garnet's attempt to justify his "equivocations" when asked about participation in the conspiracy against King James. See Shakespeare, *Macbeth* (Arden), pp. xx–xxii; also, p. 59, n. 9.

13. There is a certain heartbreak in this simile that links Lucifer and Macbeth. It recalls the audience to those first thrilling moments when Macbeth's captaincy saved Duncan's throne and was the hope of Malcolm. The suppressed love of Macbeth for Duncan is part of the tragedy's pathos, and even Malcolm is not immune to its bizarre magnetism.

One may hear almost a parody of Macbeth's blasphemous invocation to the powers of evil, in Malcolm's speech: " . . . had I pow'r. I should / Pour the sweet milk of concord into hell, / Uproar the universal peace, confound / All unity on earth" (4.3.109–12).

14. From i.sect.xxx, as cited in Basil Willey, *The Seventeenth Century Background* (Garden City, N.Y.; Doubleday Anchor Books, 1953), p. 60–61.

15. At the very last moment of my copy reading, Stanley Cavell's "Macbeth Appalled (II)" appeared in *Raritan* 12(3): 1–15 (Winter 1993). I can't forbear to quote his remarks on pages 3 and 4.

> Is there any good reason . . . to deny or to slight the one break in Lady Macbeth's silence on the subject of her childlessness, her assertion that she has suckled a (male) child? There may be good reason for her husband to deny or doubt it, in his considering whose it might be . . . the interesting question is what happened, in fact or in fantasy, to the child she remembers. (David Wilbern, as I recall, in a fine essay suggests in passing that her suckling is a fantasy. If so, then what is the fantasy of remembering a (fantasied) child?) And if we do not deny or slight her assertion then the fate of the child is *their* question, a fact or issue for them of a magnitude to cause the magnitude and intimacy of guilt and melancholy Macbeth begins with and Lady Macbeth ends with. Its massive unspokenness is registered by the reverse of the procedure of the recurrence of the words, namely by the dispersal or dissemination of words for birth throughout the play—*deliver, issue, breed, labour, hatch'd, bring forth.* I would like to include the punning use of *borne,* repeated by Lenox in his nervously ironic "Men must not walk too late" speech.

Cavell concludes:

> But when one is caught by the power—it will not happen predictably—of the vanished child, one may wonder even over Lady Macbeth's response upon the initial entrance to her of Macbeth, "I feel now / The future in the present," which in turn is, and is not, Macbeth's perception of history. (A sense of pregnancy, but without assurance of reproduction, may suggest the monstrous as much as it does the sterile.)

The weight of the unspoken in *Macbeth*, the pain of that child who lurks but is hardly spoken of directly, echoes as well in Cavell's further observation "that it is probably the sense of their [the Macbeths'] silence to one another about unsilenceable topics that has above all prompted critics to suggest that scenes are missing from the play . . . what is missing is not absent but is present in the play's specific ways of saying nothing, say of showing the unspeakable."

Another moment in Cavell's essay that struck me bears on his reading of the following lines:

The third element in defining the object of Macbeth's killing is Lady Macbeth's entrance to him upon his words, "I have no spur / To prick the sides of my intent, but only / Vaulting ambition, which o'erleaps itself / And falls on th' other." . . . Critics have wished to see in Macbeth's image of "overleaping" here an image of himself as the rider of a horse, mounting it or jumping it, overeagerly. I do not say this is wrong; but since Macbeth's words are that it is *his* intent whose sides are, or are not, to be pricked, there is a suggestion that he is identifying himself also as the horse (as earlier he associates himself with a wolf and later identifies himself as a baited bear); a horse by whom or by what ridden is unclear, ambiguous: perhaps it is by his ambition, perhaps by the ambition of another, so that "falling on the other" means falling to the other, to be responsible for it, but perhaps it means falling upon the other, as its casualty.

If it is indeed Lady Macbeth whom Macbeth falls on, as Cavell implies but does not state directly, there is also an sexual implication in this falling on "th' other" which "prick" alerts us to. This suggests even more painfully the frustration Macbeth feels in his marriage, the consummation that eludes him. And it may well ring in that line, I puzzled over earlier in my essay, "We'ld jump the life to come" in which he wishes to leap the unbearable present. If he "risks" overleaping in his murder, the promise of a future life everlasting, yet the stride of that monstrous "jump" he may hope, will bring him over the sexual hurdle and into Lady Macbeth's embrace.

Chapter 7. What Prospero Knows

1. Anne Righter in her "Introduction" to the Penguin edition of *The Tempest*, points this out succinctly in setting the pious Gonzalo's exclamation of joy in proper perspective.

> . . . In one voyage
> Did Claribel her husband find at Tunis,
> And Ferdinand her brother found a wife
> Where he himself was lost; Prospero his dukedom
> In a poor isle, and all of us ourselves
> When no man was his own.
>
> (5.1.208–13)

"The truth is that what Gonzalo says does not sum up the play now reaching its end. His speech would by no means be subscribed to, in fact, by most of the other characters. Miranda and even Ferdinand are too innocent to understand. Caliban, Stephano, and Trinculo understand even less. . . . As for Antonio and Sebastian, frustrated and unregenerate, they do not seem to rejoice at all, let alone in the measure proposed" (William Shakespeare, *The Tempest* [Harmondsworth: Penguin,1987], p. 37).

2. *King Lear*, F.F.5.3: 2962.
3. *King Lear*, F.F.5.3: 2949.
4. Stephen Greenblatt, *Shakespearean Negotiations, The Circulation of Social Energy in Renaissance England* (Berkeley: University of California Press, 1988), p. 143.
5. Greenblatt refers to this as "salutary anxiety"; *Shakespearean Negotiations*, p. 143. He claims that Prospero deliberately subjects himself to this anxiety. "Prospero directs this restaging not only against the others but also—even principally—against himself. That is, he arranges for the reenactment in a variety of registers and through different symbolic agents of the originary usurpation, and

in the play's most memorable yet perplexing moment, the princely artist puts himself through the paralyzing uneasiness with which he has afflicted others. The moment to which I refer is that of the interrupted wedding masque. In the midst of the climactic demonstration of Prospero's magical powers, the celebration of the paradisal 'green land' where spring comes at the very end of harvest, Prospero suddenly starts, breaks off the masque, and declares that he had 'forgot that foul conspiracy / Of the beast Caliban and his confederates / Against my life' (4.1.139–41)." Ibid., p. 144.

I can not quite assent to this. As Anne Righter has pointed out neither Sebastian nor Antonio are converted, and the notion of "conversion" hardly applies to most of the other characters. As far as Prospero's own conversion is concerned, he is a sorcerer not a Protestant divine, and the language of religion so prominent in *Macbeth* is notably absent in *The Tempest*.

6. See Bernard Knox, "*The Tempest* and the Ancient Comic Tradition," in *English Stage Comedy*. English Institute Essays, 1954, ed. W. K. Wimsatt Jr. (New York: Columbia University Press, 1955; reprint, Harmondsworth: Signet, 1987), p. 173–74: "There is more than a touch in him of the Plautine old man, the irascible *senex* (*severus, difficillis, iratus, saevus,* as Donatus describes him), who may in the end turn out to have a heart of gold, but who for the first four acts has only a noticeably short temper and a rough tongue."

7. Reuben A. Brower, *Fields of Light* (New York: Oxford University Press, 1951; reprint, Harmondsworth: Signet, 1987), p. 194.

8. See Partridge, *Shakespeare's Bawdy*, p. 135.

9. William Shakespeare, *The Tempest*, ed. Anne Righter (Harmondsworth: Penguin, 1987), p. 162.

10. Shakespeare, *The Tempest*, pp. 25–26.

11. *Macbeth*, 1.7.6.

12. *Shakespeare's Personality*, ed. Norman N. Holland, Sidney Homan, and Bernard J. Paris (Berkeley: University of California Press,1989), came to my attention only after finishing the final draft of this book. I might have quoted it throughout, but one essay, Bernard J. Paris's "*The Tempest:* Shakespeare's Ideal Solution," was too provocative to leave unanswered. Paris points out that "*The Tempest* is one of only two Shakespearean plays whose plot, as far as we know, is entirely the author's invention. It is, more than any other play, a fantasy of Shakespeare's." The critic queries, "What, we must ask, is it a fantasy of? . . . What is Prospero's magic doing for him? And for Shakespeare?" Paris answers himself: "What Prospero needs is what Hamlet could not find and what Shakespeare is trying to imagine: a way of taking revenge and remaining innocent. . . . This is a problem that only his magic can solve. *The Tempest* is above all a fantasy of innocent revenge. The revenge is Propero's, but the fantasy is Shakespeare's whose conflicting needs resemble those of his protagonist." (Ibid., pp. 210–12).

The importance of revenge and magic in *The Tempest* I assent to, but "conflicting needs" signals that the language of psychiatry will dominate the reading. There is much skillful diagnosis in *Shakespeare's Personality*. (One instance is William Kerrigan's observations in his article, "The Personal Shakespeare," p. 185, of the "testiness" of Prospero, the "oedipal stakes for a father" yet the "relative peace achieved through daughters," in Shakespeare despite his fathers' "sexual rage.") Diagnosis of Shakespeare may clarify stage action, but it can also set itself up in contradiction. Paris, in disparaging Prospero's magic, must ignore its share in the very means of drama, stage magic. "Magic is a means of achieving one's ends without effort and of transcending the limitations of the human condition. It is a

way of enforcing the neurotic claim that the mind is the supreme reality and that
the material world is subject to its dictates; indeed, it symbolizes that claim"
(Paris, "The Tempest," p. 211). Magic, may be "neurotic" in life, but certainly not
in a play that assumes that sorcery is real. For the audience watching and willing
to believe in the ability of Prospero to work events and summon fantastic creatures, is not magic the very "reality" that Paris regards as a "problem"? The question of why the magic did not work before has many possible answers, none of
them connected with neurosis. Obviously Prospero, when he first took up magical studies, was not skilled enough in them to see what his brother was up to.
Prospero, moreover, did not have Ariel at his disposal. Even magic, as Prospero
understands, has limitations. It can not transform human beings, neither his
brother, Antonio, nor Caliban. (Although Sherman Hawkins argues in "Aggression and the Histories," p. 65, that "Prospero's transforming art is not entirely
illusion, for by its dramaturgic working Alonso repents, Ferdinand learns, and
even Caliban is impelled to seek for grace.") In criticizing if not debunking magic,
Paris is reading a different play like The Alchemist, where indeed magic and al-
chemy have no reality. In The Tempest magic has reality, and it vies with human
nature as the supreme reality throughout.

Paris, however, does consider magic real when it serves his diagnosis of Prospero as a man deep in "neurosis." Witness, the following: "Prospero is a cunning
and sadistic revenger, who employs his magic to inflict terrible psychological violence on his enemies while he shields them from physical injury and thereby
preserves his innocence. To his thinking, as long as no one is physically injured,
'there's no harm done' (1.2.15). Prospero finds harmless such things as having
everyone, including the good Gonzalo, fear imminent destruction, having them
run mad with terror at Ariel's apparitions, and having Ferdinand and Alonso
believe each other dead" (Paris, "The Tempest," p. 214).

Who is blameless in this crew, apart from the sailors who we may safely say are
cartoons and, therefore, no more the butt of sadism than Mickey Mouse creatures? Except for Ferdinand, soon to be handsomely rewarded for his "psychological suffering," everyone, even the good Gonzalo, who has acquiesced in the
evils of his master's reign, has had a share in the possible murder of Prospero.

Caliban is a monster "more sinned against than sinning," in Paris's reading.
"Prospero exhibits a major contradiction in his attitude toward Caliban. He feels
that Caliban is subhuman, but he holds him morally responsible for his act and
punishes him severely. If Caliban in fact is subhuman, then he is not morally
responsible and should simply be kept away from Miranda, a precaution Prospero could easily effect. If he is a moral agent, then he needs to be show the error
of his ways; but Prospero's punishments are merely designed to torture him and
to break his spirit. The contradiction in Prospero's attitude results from conflicting psychological needs" (Ibid, pp. 215–16).

The events described as contradictory, however, take place in time. We are
watching human beings but also as creatures clearly fantastic. Prospero does treat
Caliban with trust and love at first. When Caliban proves to be both untrustwor-
thy and subhuman, he has to be both watched and educated. The play will educate Caliban who learns by the drunken example of his two confederates that
there is a difference between Prospero and other men. What use Caliban will
put such a lesson to is unknown, just as Antonio's end is ambiguous. To subject
Prospero's treating of the child of a fully magical witch, Caliban, and a wisp of
the air like Ariel to fine points of civil rights without acknowledging their magical
substance is to miss the spirit of The Tempest. I don't see any "contradiction" in

Prospero's behavior toward Caliban, only a magician's frustration at the limits of his power. Spirits can be good or evil in *The Tempest*, just as human characters.

Paris argues Caliban's poetry, his sensitivity, "The isle is full of noises," as proofs of his morality, but Shakespeare's villains are often endearing, sensitive. If Caliban will "seek for grace," so will Claudius. It may be Prospero's omnipotence not his "sadism" that most irritates the modern critic. When Prospero says to Antonio, "I do forgive thee, / Unnatural though thou art" (5.1. 78–79), the link to Caliban is clear enough. Both are inhuman, both are monsters. This is not condescension, it is definition. To say that "Prospero's forgiveness seems compulsive, indiscriminate, and dangerous," is to step outside the play and assume that the characters can live a life beyond it free from the restraints of the magic which has a reality in it.

> Hamlet's problem, as I see it, is how to take revenge and remain innocent. The problem is insoluble and nearly drives him mad. . . . In *The Tempest*, through Prospero's magic, he [Shakespeare] imagines a solution to Hamlet's problem: Prospero is at once vindictive and noble, vengeful and innocent. Although he takes his revenge through his magic, by raising a tempest and inflicting various psychological torments, he does not really "hurt" anybody; and when he has had his vindictive triumph, he renounces his magic and forgives everyone.
>
> *The Tempest* offers an ideal solution to the problem of how to cope with wrongs without losing one's innocence—but only through the first four acts. The solution collapses when Prospero renounces his magic, for his magic was the only means by which he could reconcile his conflicts and keep evil under control. He does not at the end seem to have attained psychological balance, or to have discovered a viable way of living in the real world.
>
> (Ibid., p. 223)

Why should Prospero live in the "real world" when "magic" is so much more attractive? "A viable way of living," for a man bent on the other world, and a wizard to boot? This is like condemning Haroun-El-Rashid for going around in beggars' rags or Sinbad the Sailor for sailing. Nor I do I see "evil" out of "control" at the end.

I agree with Paris when he draws the parallel to Prince Hamlet's revenge and the touch of the "vindictive" in Prospero's character. When Paris finds Prospero wanting in "psychological balance," however, I feel as if the critic has wandered through a proscenium arch, of nineteenth century "naturalism" where "magic" would be a problem.

Paris goes on:

> We see Prospero at the end in the grip of self-effacing and detached trends that do not promise to make him an effective ruler. Even so "sentimental" a critic as Northrop Frye observes that Prospero "appears to have been a remarkably incompetent Duke of Milan, and not to be promising much improvement after he returns. . . ." There have been many misgivings about Prospero's forgiveness of Antonio as well as doubts about his ability to cope upon their return to Italy. The forgiveness, as we have seen, is compulsive and indiscriminate. There is no evidence of repentance on Antonio's part and no reason to think that he will meekly submit to Prospero's rule. Antonio should, at the least, be put in jail; but Prospero can neither do this nor, we suspect, keep him under control. . . .
> At the end of *The Tempest* Shakespeare seems back where he started in the plays about Henry VI, with a nobly Christian ruler who cannot cope with the harsh realities of life. (Ibid., p. 224).

This ignores both the deliberate breaking of illusions at the end of the play and Shakespeare's careful denouement of *The Tempest*'s story.

Paris has previously declared that Prospero "gives up his magic because he needs to place himself in a humble position and to show that he has not used his power for personal aggrandizement but only to set things right, to bring about moral growth and reconciliation," (Ibid., p. 221). This may be so, but, as Paris admits, Prospero also surrenders magic because he has achieved his ends insofar as "magic" can achieve them. Understanding the limitations of magic is part of *The Tempest*'s wisdom. What is obvious to an audience, however, is that Prospero gives up his magic because the drama is about to end, and the magic of the play will soon be over, dispelled. Playing on this stage irony is triply effective if Shakespeare is resigning his career at this moment, and so a host of critics have suspected. The "self-effacement" of Prospero both before the epilogue and in it, where, as its leading actor, he begs for applause is surely ironic and perhaps more a palliative to the glamorizing of a wizard, than an act of humility.

I don't deny the shades that flicker through Prospero's actions on the stage. Shakespeare has deliberately indicated a severe, even unsympathetic aspect in the sorcerer. As other essays in *Shakespeare's Personality* indicate, it's possible that these reflect traits of the playwright himself, the need to control "aggression," etc., but such suppositions must be regarded with suspicion when they do not reflect what happens on the stage. Prospero's anger, his sudden shifts of mood, make him mysterious. Mystery, like magic, is the touchstone of *The Tempest*, and, without it, Prospero could not be the sorcerer he is.

Paris feels as I do the strange dark light at the end of the play and the presence of death. It is the "harsh realities" of Prospero's exit to the *other world* that footnotes the self-abasement of this otherwise proud, vindictive man, "Who is regarded, who is esteemed, who is distinguished, before the Angel of Death?" The death rattle of Rabbi Nachman before his horrified students in Babylon's *Talmud* echoes in Shakespeare's farewell.

Has Prospero not dealt with "harsh realities" in *this world*, as Paris claims? Prospero has basically settled the issue of power in Milan by arranging a dynastic marriage between his daughter Miranda and the son of the king of Naples. The marriage implies that Ferdinand will be Prospero's successor. This makes Ferdinand's father, Alonso, king of Naples, a guardian or guarantor of Prospero's realm, so that there may be an orderly succession. Prospero's competence, then, is not really an issue, and, in the act of resigning his magic, he is also resigning most of his power as well. He is in the position of King Lear at the beginning of that drama, but much more fortunately placed in that he has found a single worthy successor. Is there an echo of *Hamlet*? Prince Hamlet, indeed, should have been in position to succeed his father before the latter's death. The Ghost's carelessness in establishing his son's succession leads to the ensuing tragedy of his wife and son's death. It is a carelessness that may have led to the initial tragedy of old Hamlet's murder? "In this regard" the earlier play has an ironic coda in *The Tempest* though its final starlight mutes our laughter.

Again the magic dissolved at the end of the play, has also resolved the play. To plot the play further and wonder how Prospero's reign will "prosper" is as futile as wondering whether it will occur to Ferdinand that Miranda offered herself too easily, or whether this prince of Naples will begin to resent his father-in-law for making him cart wood and begin to harass his wife.

Chapter 8. Shakespeare's Myth

1. One can read this tendency earlier on in the essay on *Hamlet* which these lines come from; Shakespeare becomes Hamlet and Hamlet, Everyman. "Hamlet

is a name; his speeches and sayings but the idle coinage of the poet's brain. What then, are they not real? They are as real as our own thoughts. Their reality is in the reader's mind. It is *we* who are Hamlet. This play has a prophetic truth, which is above that of history. Whoever has become thoughtful and melancholy through his own mishaps or those of others; whoever has born about with him the clouded brow of reflection, and thought himself 'too much i'th' sun'; whoever has seen the golden lamp of day dimmed by envious mists rising in his own breast, and could find in the world before him only a dull blank with nothing left remarkable in it . . ."; William Hazlitt, *The Characters of Shakespear's Plays*, 2d ed. (London: Taylor & Hessey, 1818,] reprint, New York: Signet, 1963), pp. 196–97. This is Hamlet as Bartleby the Scrivener, or Noman.

2. See, for instance, Robert Lamberton, *Hesiod* (New Haven: Yale University Press, 1988), p. 2:

> . . . the shepherd Hesiod survived, a historical entity whose place in the history books was as secure as that of any other personage of the archaic period.
>
> In the past generation or two, however, research on the nature of oral tradition has severely reduced our ability to regard that figure as historical, and much that could have been said with confidence about Hesiod fifty years ago has now only the status of lost certainties.

E. R. Dodds, on the other hand, seems to regard Hesiod as a person, not a collection of poems with a personality determined by a cult center as Lamberton suggests, wishing to enhance its status as the place of the poems. "It is doubtless no accident that the first Greek to preach divine justice was Hesiod—'the helots' poet,' as King Cleomenes called him, and a man who had himself smarted under 'crooked judgments.' Nor is it accidental that in this age the doom overhanging the rich and powerful becomes so popular a theme with poets—in striking contrast to Homer, for whom, as Murray has observed, the rich men are apt to be specially virtuous"; E. R. Dodds, *The Greeks and the Irrational* (Boston: Beacon Press, 1957), p. 45. Dodds is more skeptical about a historical Homer, but, as the material just quoted indicates, Homer too is conveniently made personal, since Dodds senses a distinct point of view.

3. Yet even Dante's use of myth is subversive of fixed belief, and curiously modern, as the Polish poet, Milosz, remarks,

> . . . in this respect Dante's *Inferno* is a disturbing work. A poem written in an Age of Faith might be presumed to desist from "fictionalizing" otherworldly figures. Yet Dante teems with figures borrowed from mythology and the literature of antiquity, so that a reader seeking genuine communion with a "medieval mind" soon realizes that he has been duped: figures whose reality a medieval poet would find credible are joined with others that, from a Christian point of view, are patently fictional. Dante's *Inferno* suggests, finally, that we really do no know what it is "to believe" or "not to believe" in someone or something, that the human mind eludes a facile division into "the real" and "the imaginary," "the literal" and "the figurative." Why else did the Middle Ages indulge in *les diableries*, in those profanations staged at Shrovetide by throngs of horned, long tailed devils?" (Czeslaw Milosz, *The Land of Ulro*, trans. Louis Iribarne [New York: Farrar, Straus, Giroux, 1984], pp. 130–31.)

4. See Buber's remark: "The *melekh* gods of West Semitic tribes are fond of child sacrifice; if they wish to gain the favor of their gods in some extraordinary situation, and especially in the hour of great danger (2 Kgs. 3:26), they make payment to them with the offering of the first born" (Martin Buber, *The Prophetic Faith*, trans. Carlyle Witton-Davies [New York: Harper Torchbooks, 1960], p. 91).

Works Cited

Booth, Stephen. *King Lear, Macbeth, Indefinition & Tragedy.* New Haven: Yale University Press, 1983.

Borges, Jorge Luis. *Labyrinths.* New York: New Directions, 1964.

Brower, Reuben A. "The Mirror of Analogy." In *Fields of Light.* New York: Oxford University Press, 1951. Reprinted in *The Tempest,* edited by Robert Langbaum. Harmondsworth: Signet, 1987.

Buber, Martin. *The Prophetic Faith.* Translated by Carlyle Witton-Davies. New York: Harper Torchbooks, 1960.

Campbell, Lily B. "Macbeth: A Study in Fear." In *Shakespeare's Tragic Heroes.* New York: Barnes and Noble, 1967.

Campbell, Oscar James, and Edward G. Quinn. *The Reader's Encyclopedia of Shakespeare.* New York: Crowell, 1966.

Cassuto, U. *A Commentary on the Book of Genesis.* Part One. *From Adam to Noah.* Translated by Israel Abrahams. Jerusalem: Magnes Press, 1972.

Cavell, Stanley. "Macbeth Appalled (II)." *Raritan* 12, no. 3 (Winter 1993): 1–15.

Coleridge, Samuel Taylor. "The Lectures of 1811–1812, Lecture 12." In *Shakespearean Criticism.* 2d ed. Edited by Thomas Middleton Raysor. 2 vols. New York: Dutton and Company, Inc., 1960. Reprinted in *Hamlet,* edited by Edward Hubler. New York: Signet, 1963.

Dodds, E. R. *The Greeks and the Irrational.* University of California, 1951. Reprint. Boston: Beacon Press, 1957.

Eliot, T. S. "Hamlet and His Problems." *Selected Essays, New Edition.* New York: Harcourt, Brace & World, 1950. Reprinted in *Twentieth Century Interpretations of Hamlet,* edited by David Bevington. Englewood Cliffs, N.J.: Prentice-Hall, 1968.

Greenblatt, Stephen. *Shakespearean Negotiations, The Circulation of Social Energy in Renaissance England.* Berkeley: University of California Press, 1988.

Harbage, Alfred. "Introduction." *Macbeth.* The Pelican Shakespeare. Baltimore: Penguin, 1956.

Hawkins, Sherman. "Aggression and the Histories," In *Shakespeare's Personality,* edited by Norman N. Holland, Sidney Homan, and Bernard J. Paris. Berkeley: University of California, 1989.

Hazlitt, William. *The Characters of Shakespear's Plays.* 2d ed. London: Taylor & Hessey, 1818. Reprinted in *Hamlet,* edited by Edward Hubler. New York: Signet, 1963.

Holland, Norman N., Sidney Homan, and Bernard J. Paris, eds. *Shakespeare's Personality.* Berkeley: University of California, 1989.

Jenkins, Harold. "Introduction and Notes." *Hamlet.* The Arden Shakespeare. Routledge: London, 1990.

Jones, Ernest. *Hamlet and Oedipus.* Norton. 1949. Reprint. Garden City, N.Y.: Anchor Books, 1954.

Kerrigan, William. "The Personal Shakespeare: Three Clues." In *Shakespeare's Personality,* edited by Norman N. Holland, Sidney Homan, and Bernard J. Paris. Berkeley: University of California, 1989.

Knox, Bernard. "*The Tempest* and the Ancient Comic Tradition." In *English Stage Comedy.* English Institute Essays, 1954, edited by W. K. Wimsatt Jr. New York: Columbia University Press, 1955. Reprinted in *The Tempest,* edited by Robert Langbaum. Harmondsworth: Signet, 1987.

Lamberton, Robert. *Hesiod.* New Haven: Yale University Press, 1988.

Levin, Harry. *The Question of Hamlet.* New York: Oxford University Press, 1978.

McCarthy, Mary. *Occasional Pieces.* San Diego: Harcourt Brace Jovanovich, 1985.

Mack, Maynard. "The World of *Hamlet.*" *Yale Review* 41 (1952): Reprinted in *Hamlet,* edited by Edward Hubler. New York: Signet, 1963.

Milosz, Czeslaw. *The Land of Ulro.* Translated by Louis Iribarne. New York: Farrar, Straus, Giroux, 1984.

Paris, Bernard J. "*The Tempest:* Shakespeare's Ideal Solution," In *Shakespeare's Personality,* edited by Norman N. Holland, Sidney Homan, and Bernard J. Paris. Berkeley: University of California, 1989.

Partridge, Eric. *Shakespeare's Bawdy.* New York: Dutton, 1960.

Righter, Anne. "Introduction." *The Tempest.* The New Penguin Shakespeare. Harmondsworth: Penguin, 1987.

Shakespeare, William. *Hamlet.* With an Introduction by W. W. Greg. First Quarto, 1603. Shakespeare Quarto Facsimiles, no. 7. Oxford: Clarendon Press, n.d.

———. *Hamlet.* With an Introduction by W. W. Greg. Second Quarto 1604–5. Shakespeare Quarto Facsimiles, no. 4. Oxford: At the Clarendon Press, 1940. Reprint. With an Introduction by Charlton Hinman. Oxford: Oxford University Press, 1964.

———. *Hamlet.* Edited by Charlton Hinman. The Norton Facsimile: The First Folio of Shakespeare. New York: W. W. Norton, 1968.

———. *Hamlet.* Edited by Edward Hubler. New York: Signet, 1963.

———. *Hamlet.* Edited by Harold Jenkins. The Arden Shakespeare. Routledge: London, 1990.

———. *Hamlet.* Edited by Louis B. Wright and Virginia A. LaMar. The Folger Library Shakespeare. New York: Pocket Books, 1958.

———. *King Lear.* Edited by Kenneth Muir. The Arden Shakespeare. Routledge: London, 1990.

———. *Macbeth.* Edited by Louis B. Wright and Virginia A. LaMar. The Folger Library Shakespeare. New York: Pocket Books, 1959.

———. *Macbeth.* Edited by Kenneth Muir. The Arden Shakespeare. London: Routledge, 1989.

———. *Macbeth.* Edited by Alfred Harbage. The Pelican Shakespeare. Baltimore: Penguin, 1956.

———. *The Tempest.* Edited by Robert Langbaum. Harmondsworth: Signet, 1987.

———. *The Tempest.* Edited by Anne Righter. The New Penguin Shakespeare. Harmondsworth: Penguin, 1987.

————. *The Parallel King Lear.* Prepared by Michael Warren. Berkeley: University of California Press, 1989.

Twentieth Century Interpretations of Hamlet. Edited by David Bevington. Englewood Cliffs, N.J.: Prentice Hall, 1968.

Urkowitz, Steven. "Burying Three Hamlets." In *Shakespeare Study Today.* Edited by Georgianna Ziegler. New York: AMS Press, 1986.

————. *Shakespeare's Revision of King Lear.* Princeton: Princeton University Press, 1980.

Willey, Basil. *The Seventeenth Century Background.* Garden City, N.Y.: Doubleday Anchor Books, 1953.

Wimsatt, W. K. Jr., ed. *English Stage Comedy.* English Institute Essays, 1954. New York: Columbia University Press, 1955.

Yeats, W. B. "Crazy Jane Talks With the Bishop." In *The Collected Poems of W. B. Yeats.* New York: The Macmillan Company, 1958.

Ziegler, Georgianna, ed. *Shakespeare Study Today.* New York: AMS Press, 1986.

Index

composition, 99; riddle of the child, 100–104, 107–8, 110, 112, 114–17; self-analysis, 16; sexual impotence, 104, 111, 113–14, 116–17, 159 n.4, 162 n.15; women in, 104–8, 146, 161 n.6

Mack, Maynard, 154 n.20
McCarthy, Mary, 147 n.4
Milosz, Czeslaw, 168 n.3
Muir, Kenneth, 162 n.12

Nothing and zero: in *Hamlet*, 77–78, 95, 97; in *King Lear*, 20, 31, 36–39, 46; in *Macbeth*, 122; as nihilism, 150 n.7; in *The Tempest*, 127, 130

Olivier, Laurence: acting of King Lear, 21, 30; direction of movie *Hamlet*, 67, 74, 85, 96, 155 n.2, 158 n.10
Other world: in *King Lear*, 28, 30–32, 44; in *Hamlet*, 50–54, 56–57, 62, 65–67, 70, 74, 84–85, 95, 161 n.7; in *Macbeth*, 99, 105–6, 109, 110–11, 119–21, 161 nn. 7 and 12; in *The Tempest*, 125–27, 133–36, 138
Ozick, Cynthia, 145

Partridge, Eric, 149 n.3, 150 n.4
Pirandello, Luigi, 60

Quinn, Edward, 17, 147 n.2, 153 n.9

Religious myth, 51, 81, 74, 119, 120, 141–46, 168 n.3. *See also* Biblical echoes; Greek myth
Righter, Anne, 137, 163 n.1

Secret lives, 42, 44–45
Sexual reference: breast, 36, 40, 79, 80, 102, 103, 106; ditch, bed, and grave, 23, 26, 27, 41, 45, 54, 66, 45, 66, 91, 103, 109, 116, 130–31, 133–36, 139, 146; fantasy and desire in *Hamlet*, 56, 75–81, 91, 156 nn. 3 and 5; fantasy and desire in *King Lear*, 20–27, 33–42, 45; fantasy and desire in *Macbeth*, 109, 111–12, 114–16, 161 n.6, 162 n.15; fantasy and desire in *The Tempest*, 128–29, 130, 133, 134–36, 139; incest, 143 (*see also Hamlet; King*

Lear; The Tempest: incestuous desire); impotence, 104; male organ, 24, 45, 76, 80, 81, 86, 178, 149 n.3; poopies, 79–80, 156 n.4; vagina, 26, 27, 28, 36, 39, 40, 77–78, 129, 150 n.3; virginity, 80, 134–36, 139, 157 n.8. See also *Macbeth:* sexual impotence; women in

Shakespeare, William: absence in, 15–17, 47, 55, 62, 68, 100, 143; anger, 47–70, 138; anguish in being a father, 144, 146, 151 n.2, 164 n.12; autobiography of, 15–17, 20, 99, 122–23, 136, 139, 141, 145–46, 147 n.2, 167 n.12; female nature, 57, 104, 106–8, 121, 146; heirs, 104–5, 107, 110–11, 115, 117, 123, 136–37, 146, 159 n.3, 160 n.5, 161 n.7; playing Ghost, 147 n.2; revision of plays, 17, 19, 31, 33–46, 50–52, 57–59, 64, 71–97 (*see also* Urkowitz, Steven); son, Hamnet, 104, 117, 147 n.2; uneasiness, 44, 60, 125, 139, 164 n.12; use of myth, 141–46. See also *Hamlet; King Lear; Macbeth; The Tempest:* childlessness

Sophocles: *Oedipus Rex*, 56, 141–43, 144
Sphinx, the, 142
Suicide: in *Hamlet*, 42–43, 49, 52, 55, 61, 71, 87, 88, 121, 153 n.16, 154 n.18, 157–58 n.8; in *King Lear*, 42–43, 108; in *Macbeth*, 108, 121

Tempest, The: anxiety in, 125, 127–28, 130, 132, 138–39, 163 n.5; childlessness, 132, 146; control, 125, 164 n.12; death in, 132, 136; dream in, 125, 127, 137–39; freedom and slavery, 136; idyll and paradise, 133–36, 138–39; incestuous desire, 125, 128–31, 142; magic in, 164 n.12; Miranda's inattention, 132–33; Miranda's virginity, 134–36, 139; parallels with *Hamlet* and *King Lear*, 128, 138, 166 n.12, 167 n.12; parallels with *Macbeth*, 138; Prospero's anger, 138; time in, 16, 125–126, 133, 137–39; use of "wench," 129; utopia, 133–36, 138–39
Theological protest: in Dante, 168 n.3; in *Hamlet*, 81; in *King Lear*, 15, 45, 118, 147 n.4, 150 n.7; in *Macbeth*, 110,